DEATH OF
SOMOZA

Claribel Alegría
and
Darwin Flakoll

CURBSTONE PRESS

First Edition, 1996. Reprinted in 2006.
Copyright © 1996 Claribel Alegría and Darwin Flakoll
ALL RIGHTS RESERVED

Printed in the U.S. on acid-free paper by BookMobile
Cover design: Les Kanturek

Curbstone Press is a 501(c)(3) nonprofit publishing house whose operations are supported in part by private donations and by grants. This book was published with the support of the Connecticut Commission on the Arts, National Endowment for the Arts, and donations from many individuals. We are very grateful for this support.

Library of Congress Cataloging-in-Publication Data

Alegría, Claribel.
    Death of Somoza / by Claribel Alegría and Darwin J. Flakoll.
        p.   cm.
    Based on interviews conducted in 1983 with the commando team which carried out the assassination of deposed Nicaraguan President Somoza in Asunción, Paraguay.
    ISBN 1-880684-26-8
    1. Somoza, Anastasio, 1925-1980—Assassination. 2. Asunción (Paraguay)—History.   I. Flakoll, Darwin J.   II. Title.
F1527.S6A53   1996
989.2' 121—dc20   95-36159

published by
CURBSTONE PRESS   321 Jackson Street   Willimantic, CT 06226
e-mail: info@curbstone.org   WWW.curbstone.org

To the memory of
Rigoberto López Pérez
and
Hugo Alfredo Irurzún

The tree of liberty is nourished
with the blood of tyrants.
—Thomas Jefferson

Cuan Kang asked Mencius the following:

"I have heard that Tang exiled Emperor Kie and that Wu Wang assassinated Emperor Cheu. Are these things true?"

"History assures us they are," Mencius replied.

"But," the king continued, "may a subject kill the prince?"

"He who outrages humanity," responded the philosopher, "is called an assassin, and he who outrages justice, a villain. Assassins and villains are the excrement of the human species. I have heard it said that Wu Wang killed a man named Cheu, but not that he killed the prince."

—Colloquies of Mencius

TIME CAPSULE
— Document —

"Conclusions" from the OAS *Report on the Situation of Human
Rights in Nicaragua* (1978)

In the light of the foregoing, the Inter-American Commission on
Human Rights, in plenary, has arrived at the conclusion that the
Government of Nicaragua has incurred responsibility for the
following serious, persistent, and generalized violations:

a) The Government of Nicaragua is responsible for serious attempts
against the right to life, in violation of the international humani-
tarian norms, in repressing, in an excessive and disproportionate
manner, the insurrections that occurred last September in the main
cities of the country. In fact, the bombing of towns by the National
Guard was done in an indiscriminate fashion and without prior
evacuation of the civilian population, which caused innumerable
deaths of persons who were not involved in the conflict, and, in
general, a dramatic situation;

b) Likewise, the Government of Nicaragua is responsible for a large
number of deaths which occurred after the combats, because of
abuses perpetrated by the National Guard during the so-called
"Operation Mop-up" and other actions several days after the cessa-
tion of hostilities, in which many persons were executed in a sum-
mary and collective fashion for the mere reason of living in neighborhoods or districts where there had been activity by the Frente
Sandinista de Liberación Nacional (FSLN); and young people and
defenseless children were killed;

c) The Government of Nicaragua has obstructed the work of the Red
Cross by not allowing it to carry out its responsibilities during the
combat: caring for the wounded, picking up bodies, and its humani-
tarian mission in general. Moreover, the Government is responsible
for the death of two Red Cross corpsmen and the improper use of
local ambulances and the emblem of the Red Cross;

d) The Government of Nicaragua is also responsible for the death and serious abuse, arbitrary detention, and other violations of the human rights of peasant groups;

e) In the events of last September and even earlier, there were serious violations to the right to personal security, by means of tortures and other physical abuses which were inflicted on numerous detainees;

f) A special situation, which deeply concerned the Commission, is the one dealing with minors. Aside from the many youths who are being detained in jails, along with common delinquents, the Commission was able to prove a general repression by the National Guard against any male youth between 14 and 21 years of age;

g) The physical liberty of the people is seriously affected, as is evidenced by the many arbitrary detentions that occurred early in September, the number of which increased after constitutional guarantees were suspended. This situation, furthermore, is aggravated by the administration of the judicial system which exists in Nicaragua, and by the powers enjoyed by Police Judges, some of whom are also Commanders of the National Guard, who may impose penalties of up to six months of jail, without any procedure other than listening to the accused, and by the powers of the military courts to judge civilians during periods of emergency. The foregoing shows that there have been violations to the right of protection against arbitrary detention and to due process, and, in particular, to the right to an adequate defense;

h) The freedom of expression of opinions is severely restricted when in fact information about events occurring in Nicaragua is limited to newspapers, radio and TV stations which are controlled, either directly or indirectly, by the Government. In the case of the written or spoken media independent of or in opposition to the Government, even when there was no censorship, their owners, directors or journalists were subjected to serious attempts on or threats to their lives, freedom, or security;

i) Although there is a formal respect for the freedom of conscience, worship, and religion, in practice these cannot be fully enjoyed due to the abuse, in words and deeds, to which priests and ministers of the various Catholic congregations have been subjected;

j) At present the right to assembly cannot be exercised. Even before the emergency regime came into effect, the right to association, in general, and those of political and trade union associations, in particular, had been seriously limited;

k) The right to vote has been hindered by various obstructions of a practical and legal nature which limit its free exercise.

The violations to human rights included in this report have affected all sectors of the Nicaraguan population. Its victims are and have been especially those persons of limited economic resources and young people between the ages of 14 and 21.

The damage and suffering caused by these violations have awakened, in a very forceful way, an intense and general feeling among Nicaraguan people for the establishment of a system which will guarantee the observance of human rights.

CDH/1243

PREFACE

It was in the aftermath of the blundering Malvinas invasion, a self-inflicted debacle which dealt the death blow to the Argentine military dictatorship, that we met Ramón and he invited us to write the definitive account of the bringing to justice of Anastasio Somoza Debayle. During the following months, with his help, we were able to make contact with all the survivors of the commando team that carried out the operation in Asunción, Paraguay.

By the time we finished transcribing the lengthy interviews, pieced together the entire suspense-filled plot and produced the first draft of this manuscript, the Argentine dictatorship had collapsed and a democratic Argentina had emerged on the world scene under the aegis of President Raúl Alfonsín.

Ramón materialized out of the blue once again and asked us to postpone publication of the book, inasmuch as the Revolutionary Workers' Party (PRT) had opted for a line of peaceful political action in conjunction with other leftist groups to achieve the changes it deemed necessary in Argentina. In this new situation, he explained, he did not want the PRT or its armed wing, the People's Revolutionary Army (ERP) to be unnecessarily tarred as a terrorist group.

We complied with his request because we could understand that publication of the manuscript at that time, the end of 1983, might foment polemics and recriminations best laid aside in a country that was seeking to restore an image of civility. In brief, we placed the manuscript on a closet shelf and left it to gather dust for the next five years.

At the beginning of 1989 we took it down, blew the dust off and began to think of publishing it once more. It was at this juncture that we were stunned to read of the attack on *La Tablada* fortress in Buenos Aires by an armed group of Argentine leftists led by Ramón. The newspaper accounts were confused, contradictory and, to us, inexplicable. By this time we had long since lost contact with all members of the commando team, including Ramón himself, and we decided unilaterally to return the manuscript to the shelf and leave it there.

Now, in 1993, however, the *La Tablada* episode is a dwindling footnote in history, and we decided the time had come to publish this definitive account of how Anastasio Somoza Debayle was brought to justice. The book you hold in your hands is not an apology for terrorism, but rather the chronicle of a tyrannicide.

The authors
Managua, Nicaragua
July, 1993

DEATH OF
SOMOZA

.

CHAPTER 1

President Anastasio Somoza Debayle presented his resignation to an emergency session of the Nicaraguan Congress in the Rubén Darío Salon of the Intercontinental Hotel shortly after midnight on July 17, 1979. The resignation, dated July 16, was badly typed in capital letters on a sheet of presidential stationery. It read:

HONORABLE NATIONAL CONGRESS
PEOPLE OF NICARAGUA

AFTER CONSULTATION WITH GOVERNMENTS THAT HAVE TRUE INTEREST IN PACIFYING THE COUNTRY, I HAVE DECIDED TO RESPECT THE DISPOSITION OF THE ORGANIZATION OF AMERICAN STATES, AND I TAKE THIS MEANS TO RESIGN FROM THE PRESIDENCY TO WHICH I WAS ELECTED BY POPULAR VOTE. MY RESIGNATION IS IRREVOCABLE.

I HAVE FOUGHT AGAINST COMMUNISM, AND I BELIEVE THAT WHEN THE TRUTH COMES OUT, HISTORY WILL VINDICATE ME.

A. SOMOZA
PRESIDENT OF THE REPUBLIC

There was no legal quorum of Congress present to accept his resignation or to elect his constitutional successor, Francisco Urcuyo Maliaño, because a majority of the deputies and senators had already fled to Miami to escape the impending debacle. During the past several weeks, top officials, cabinet ministers, and legislators of the Somoza government had taken up residence in the Intercontinental Hotel—the only place in Managua where their security could be guaranteed in the face of the popular insurrection, led by the Sandinista National Liberation Front (FSLN), that was sweeping the country.

After delivering his resignation to Congress, Somoza canceled his televised farewell address to the nation and disappeared into his supposedly impregnable "bunker" atop the low hill of Tiscapa, a few blocks from the hotel. Here he finished packing, leaving unmade beds and items of clothing scattered about the presidential bedroom, while Urcuyo Maliaño was sworn in and adorned with the presidential sash at 1:52 in the morning. At 4:30 Somoza climbed into a helicopter and was flown to Las Mercedes airport on the outskirts of Managua, where three getaway planes were awaiting him and members of his entourage. Top military and civilian officials of the crumbling regime boarded a Dehavilland 125/600 and a Convair 880 and took off in a northerly direction. In the baggage compartment of the Convair, surrounded by a jumble of bags and suitcases, were two zinc coffins containing the remains of the dictator's father, Anastasio Somoza García, and his elder brother, Luis Somoza, both of whom had preceded Anastasio II in the presidency.

At the last moment, eight gaily-colored parrots from the dictator's private zoo were loaded, incongruously, into his plane, a Lear jet, and the craft took off at 5:10, bringing an end to the Somoza dynasty's forty-three-year reign in Nicaragua.

"Tachito" Somoza, as he was called to distinguish him from the dynasty's founder, "Tacho," left behind him a ravaged, bankrupt nation. The FSLN's unsuccessful insurrection of September 1978 and its victorious final offensive that began seven weeks earlier, had left a death toll of 50,000, 80 percent of them civilians killed by Somoza's indiscriminate air bombardment of six major cities in a vain attempt to keep the Sandinista guerrillas from consolidating power. It also left in its wake 100,000 wounded, an estimated 40,000 orphans and 150,000 Nicaraguan refugees in the neighboring countries of Honduras and Costa Rica.

During the final days, when he realized that his downfall was inevitable, Somoza and his closest associates systematically siphoned off all the loose cash in the country, leaving the Central

Bank with reserves of only the 3 million dollars he was unable to lay his hands on. It was a sum sufficient to keep the country running for two days. In their systematic strip-mining of Nicaragua, not only had Somoza and his cronies mortgaged their extensive agricultural and commercial/industrial holdings to the hilt, but Somoza had also run up a foreign debt of 1.6 billion dollars which, in the words of a subsequent CEPAL economic analysis, "was not destined to foment the economic and social development of Nicaragua, but rather to free internal resources so they could be taken out of the country."

The looting of Nicaragua was a long-established family tradition, inaugurated by Tacho I, first Director-in-Chief of the U.S.-created National Guard. The elder Somoza consolidated his grip on power by treacherously assassinating the guerrilla chieftain, Augusto César Sandino, in February 1934 in the midst of a truce. Two years later, Anastasio Somoza García deposed Juan B. Sacasa, his uncle by marriage, from the presidency and took over undisputed political and military control of Nicaragua. He lost no time in starting to accumulate one of the largest family fortunes in Latin America.

In 1944, *Time* correspondent William Krehm investigated the Somoza family resources and came up with the following partial list:

> ...the private sale of cattle to Panama; the clandestine sale of cattle to Costa Rica; a monopoly on the distribution of tallow; the pasteurizing plant, "La Salud," in Managua; ownership of the gold mine, "San Albino;" an extra income of 175,000 dollars a year from an "additional contribution" of 2.25% of the production of North American mining companies; ownership of 51 cattle ranches; ownership of 46 coffee plantations; ownership of the huge Montelimar ranch; ownership of 50% of the shares of the Nicaraguan cement factor; ownership of 41% of the shares of the cotton mill of the Salvadoran magnate, Gadala María; ownership of 50% of the shares of the Momotombo National Match Company, whose sales were assured by prohibiting the importation of cigarette

lighters; ownership of the newspaper, *Novedades*; ownership of most of the sawmills in the country; ownership of the buildings that housed the Nicaraguan legations in Mexico and Costa Rica; ownership of various apartment houses in Miami; ownership of the electric plants in Chinandega, Tipitapa, Jinotega, Estelí, and La Libertad; ownership of Las Mercedes, the property adjoining the Managua airport...

Tacho II was a "Made in U.S.A." product who spoke English better than he did Spanish. He was educated at West Point Military Academy, where his one claim to distinction was that of being the only cadet in the history of that august institution to receive a private army as a graduation gift. On his return to Nicaragua, he began a meteoric rise through the officer corps of the National Guard, and when his father's twenty-year career of corruption and enrichment was terminated in September 1956 by three poison-tipped bullets from the revolver of a young Nicaraguan poet and newspaperman, Rigoberto López Pérez, Anastasio Somoza Debayle inherited his father's lifetime post as Director-in-Chief of the Nicaraguan National Guard. As such, and subsequently as president, he was bitterly referred to by political opponents as "the last Marine," in honor of the fact that U.S. Marines occupied Nicaragua almost continuously from 1912 until 1933, when they were evicted by Sandino, only to be replaced by local proxies—the three members of the Somoza dynasty.

It is doubtful that any such considerations occupied Anastasio Somoza Debayle's mind during that early morning flight to Homestead Air Force Base, Miami. To cite his own words, in his subsequent apologia, *Nicaragua Betrayed*:

In that flight to Miami, many thoughts ran through my mind. They mainly concerned what President Jimmy Carter and the U.S. Department of State had done in Nicaragua. In a short period of time they had destroyed what had taken thirty years to build. With a single pen stroke they had wiped out 14,000 men who had passed through U.S. military schools and who constituted the principal bulwark against communism in Central America. I felt agony.

As Somoza's plane approached its destination at the tip of Florida, Nicaragua's new president, Francisco Urcuyo Maliaño, went on the airwaves to deliver his first, and last, address to the nation. His speech stunned observers, particularly U.S. Ambassadors Lawrence Pezzullo and William Bowdler, State Department experts on Central American affairs, who had during the past weeks painstakingly negotiated a formula for the turnover of power by Somoza's successor to the revolutionary Junta waiting in the wings in San Jose, Costa Rica, that would ensure the survival of the Nicaraguan National Guard as watchdog of U.S. interests in the Central American nation.

The Somoza family newspaper, *Novedades*, in its swan song as official newspaper of the regime, reported Urcuyo's bombshell discourse under the headline, "President Urcuyo calls for conciliation":

> The President of the Republic, Dr. Francisco Urcuyo Maliaño, in his first message called on Nicaraguans to achieve reconciliation so that, united, we might begin the reconstruction of Nicaragua. The First Citizen indicated that he was assuming with full responsibility the high office with which the Honorable Congress of the Republic had invested him, adding that in his spirit there dwelt no rancor whatsoever, and that it is the obligation of all Nicaraguans to forget the past and to base themselves in the present with a view toward the future.

In another part of his important message, the President of the Republic called for a dialogue among all the political forces of the nation who share a belief in democracy.

In the same manner, Dr. Urcuyo Maliaño called on the irregular forces to put down their arms before the altar of the Fatherland...

"I wish to place in the historical record my admiration and recognition of the National Guard which has ably defended the sovereignty of the Fatherland, its territorial integrity, and the rule of the Constitution," President Urcuyo stated in the conclusion of his Inaugural Address to the people of Nicaragua.

In Washington, DC, disbelieving officials in the White House and Department of State slowly assimilated the fact that the Somoza dynasty had ended as it had begun two generations earlier: with an act of treachery. Somoza had deliberately failed to advise his inept successor, who had a long history as Congressional buffoon and court jester, that he had only been appointed president in order to turn the reins of power over to the new Sandinista government. Urcuyo's act resulted in the immediate and total disintegration of the National Guard and in his own ignominious departure from Nicaragua aboard a military plane bound for Guatemala exactly forty hours and forty-three minutes after he assumed the presidency. He was to be remembered only for his unwitting demolition of the Praetorian Guard that had served the United States and the Somoza family's interests for fifty-one years, and he was to go down in Nicaragua history books as "Urcuyo the Brief."

After disembarking at Homestead Air Force Base, Tachito Somoza was driven to his palatial mansion in Miami Beach and had not finished unpacking his luggage when the telephone rang. In *Nicaragua Betrayed*, he describes the conversation that followed:

> It was Undersecretary of State Warren Christopher with a message that was brief but indisputably clear and peremptory. Christopher told me that under the terms of the agreement with Ambassador Pezzullo I was welcome to the United States, but on the basis of the comments by the new president, that welcome had been withdrawn. Then he stated that he was speaking in the name of the highest levels in the White House. That, of course, could only be Jimmy Carter.

Once again, I was forced to confront the treachery of Jimmy Carter. I had followed the plan of the United States word for word. To assure the future of the National Guard and the Liberal Party, I had tried to adjust myself to the plan point by point. I had made all the military chiefs understand the importance of accepting faithfully and in its entirety Pezzullo's plan, and this had been accepted by General Mejía and the new General Staff. At that point I discovered that they were holding me responsible for a speech made by the new president of Nicaragua while I was en route to Miami. Mr. Carter and his Department of State were holding me responsible for things over which I had no control.

As the erstwhile dictator of Nicaragua hung up the phone to ponder where his search for a secure retreat might lead him, he had exactly fourteen months to live.

CHAPTER 2

Characteristically, it was Armando who brought matters to a head. Santiago, their one-man scouting party, had only been gone ten days, and it had been arranged that he was to make the trans-Atlantic call when he had definite news to report. But still, they had the standby number in the Panama hotel.

"Are we going to call him to find out if he's made contact with the Frente?"

The two of them were sitting in Ramón's minuscule living room in a small fishing village near Barcelona. Despite Sonia's decorating efforts—a few solidarity posters on the walls, a glass jar containing a bouquet of freshly-cut flowers on the low table between them—the room retained the starkness of an exile's temporarily-rented quarters, which is precisely what it was.

Ramón drew on his cigarette and blew smoke at the flowers. It had been a difficult two years for all of them. Moreso for Armando, who had only been released from an Argentine military prison some six months previously. Four years in prison, yet here he was, head up, his stocky body hunched forward, reminding Ramón of a veteran cavalry horse pricking up his ears at the sound of a distant bugle.

The nucleus of the team was together again, or within communications-reach of each other, after weathering the tempests of dissension and division that the enemy had carefully planted and nourished in their midst. That grueling ordeal was behind them, as well as the vicissitudes of twenty-four months of crossing European borders on false papers, of scrounging for the most menial jobs to ensure survival. Ramón himself had been a door-to-door salesman of shoddy jewelry for months in Madrid before landing a sinecure as a real estate salesman and rental commission agent in this small Catalan village that was steadily being ruined by the tourist invasion.

Not that there wasn't money. There was, and plenty of it, safely stored away in Swiss bank accounts. But that was untouchable. It was for the Revolution, and the Organization's inflexible rule was that every militant who could maintain a semblance of legality must secure his livelihood by his own means until he had no choice but to vanish underground.

Everything is relative, Ramón reflected. His present life, accompanied by his wife and two children, was a model of domestic bliss compared to the hard, hunted, death-dodging existence he had led for years before leaving Argentina nearly a year after the Videla coup and the beginning of the real repression. It was the same for the rest of them, and Ramón knew, because he occasionally felt the twinge himself, that the comparative soft living of European exile was a subtle but deadly corrosive that weakened revolutionary will, deposited fatty tissue in the interstices between the brain cells and took the edge off the split-second psychological and physical reflexes that spell the difference between life and death in clandestine existence.

Ramón mentally ticked off the list of names. He and Santiago had developed the group into a finely-tuned, highly functional machine that was now in danger of becoming rusted and unsynchronized through disuse. As Susana was to say, almost fiercely, on thinking back to the European wanderings of the team:

> They are the ones who fought for the return to the homeland, the return to Latin America, fought to keep alive our faith in the Revolution. They fought for all of that while in Europe, which was poisonous, contrary, because it promised everything beautiful while we were moving toward everything ugly, leaving with just the clothes on our backs, starting over from zero.
> "Are we going to call Santiago...?"

The question hung in the air, and Ramón drew on his cigarette again before replying.

"No," he decided abruptly. "We'll go even if we don't have a contact. At least we'll be back in Latin America."

Friendly relations between the Nicaraguan FSLN and the Argentine People's Revolutionary Army (ERP) had been established years before when Carlos Fonseca and Mario Roberto Santucho initiated the contact. Ramón had picked up the thread less than a year before when he was invited to Havana to attend the anniversary celebration of the assault on the Moncada fortress. There he had befriended Jacinto Suárez, a veteran cadre of the Sandinista organization and, still in Havana a few weeks later, the two of them listened to the news of the FSLN's successful assault on the National Palace. A 25-man commando team took the huge building in a lightning assault and held 1,500 hostages inside—including the entire Nicaraguan Congress—for two days until Tachito Somoza bowed to their demands and released all FSLN prisoners who had survived the savage tortures of the dictator's jailers.

It was then that Ramón offered the services of his group of battle-toughened Argentine revolutionaries to help the FSLN overthrow the Somoza dynasty. The Videla dictatorship was firmly installed in Argentina, and the resistance movement had been effectively crushed for the moment, but here was an opportunity to help the Latin American liberation struggle effectively, since it was apparent that the FSLN had seized the strategic initiative in Nicaragua months before when it launched its military offensive of October 1977.

Suárez agreed that Ramón's contingent of veterans would be welcome and promised that the FSLN would call on them and make arrangements for their reception at the first favorable juncture. Neither of the two foresaw the virtually spontaneous national insurrection that would follow on the heels of the assault on the National Palace. The FSLN placed itself at the head of this manifestation of popular anger against the dictatorship but lacked a coordinated national battle plan, and Somoza's National Guard was able to concentrate its elite forces against one rebellious city after another to put down the uprising within a matter of weeks.

It was not until May 1979 that the call came through, and

Ramón responded immediately by dispatching Santiago to Panama to make contact with the FSLN and arrange for reception of the rest of the group.

"I'll phone the others and tell them to get ready to move out." Ramón stubbed out his cigarette. "You call the airlines and make reservations for the first five of us for tomorrow night."

Two days later, Ramón, Armando, and three others of the group landed at Panama International Airport in the early dawn. Armando recalls their arrival:

> We arrived and checked into a fleabag hotel since we were practically broke. We met Santiago at 8 in the morning.
>
> "I have to keep an appointment," he told us. "I don't know if anyone will show up. So far I haven't had any luck."
>
> We saw him again at ten in the morning, and he had finally made contact with the Frente. We met with them, and they told us, "There's a plane loaded with medicines leaving for the Southern Front. Do you want to go along?"
>
> "Let's go!" Ramón exclaimed. He was ready to leave our bags and everything at the hotel.
>
> "No, no," they told us, "go get your bags and we'll meet you at the airport."
>
> A few hours later we landed at another airport where there were lots of people in uniform. We knew it must be on the Costa Rican border, probably Liberia. We were put up in a house for two days before they piled us into a truck at night, and we headed for the Southern Front. I remember we were with José Valdivia, and he told us:
>
> "Find yourselves a hole somewhere and crawl in because it's soon going to start raining mortar shells."
>
> We had fought guerrilla style, but never in a regular war like this. Mortar shells began dropping around us, and we didn't know where to hide. It was a terrible shock, but in a few days we got accustomed to the dynamics of the war.

Santiago, who had Argentine experience as an instructor in combat training, was assigned to a training command and spent the first several weeks on the Southern Front teaching the flood of raw recruits streaming in to join the FSLN the elements of arms handling, marksmanship, and combat tactics. Armando, who knew trucks and mechanics, was assigned to a transport command known as the Suicide Unit and was soon driving trucks laden with munitions and food to the firing line and bringing back wounded to the field hospital. Ramón recalled:

> I was near Sapoá. I didn't participate in any offensive action but simply took care that no bombs fell on me and worked at other things. There were no infantry incursions by the enemy, and we weren't ordered to attack, so it was essentially a defensive position. It was the first time we had taken part in a regular military action, with artillery, defense of fixed positions, and continual air attacks. It was a great education.

When the final offensive got underway on May 28, 1979, the Benjamín Zeledón column that launched the attack on the Southern Front, consisted of 450 troops. El Naranjo on the Pacific Coast was the first point of attack, and after stopping the counterattacking enemy forces, the FSLN column withdrew to launch a new offensive on the lake side of the narrow waist of land, taking Peñas Blancas and Sapoá and starting a northward push to threaten the strategic town of Rivas. By this time the column had increased in size to 800 troops, and Santiago and other instructors were working night and day to prepare the stream of volunteers to face the elite units of the National Guard that had been sent southward from Managua to turn back the offensive.

The FSLN high command had designed the offensive on the Southern Front to pin down Somoza's crack mobile units while the other five guerrilla fronts launched their attacks throughout the country. For seven weeks the Benjamín Zeledón column bore the brunt of the Guard's fierce counter-thrusts, blunting them one after the other and resuming its own offensive with the announced intention of capturing Rivas and installing a provisional revolutionary government there.

A long-awaited shipment of mortars and RPG-2 bazookas arrived and enormously increased the rebels' fire power. By this

time the training command was functioning smoothly, and
Santiago, who was an artillery expert as well, was assigned to an
artillery unit and joined the fighting.

The final four days of fighting on the Southern Front were the
hardest of the brief war. By this time the column had swelled to
2,000 troops, and a final enemy counteroffensive had been turned
back on July 15. In the midst of the continuing battle, troop
dispositions were made for a new thrust to pierce the Guards' line.
Arrangements were completed on the 17th, the day Somoza fled
Nicaragua for Miami, and Ramón heard the news over the radio
in the improvised command post. He remembers the thought
flashed through his mind: "The son-of-a-bitch got away. I hope
somebody kills him." But there was no one with whom to share
the sentiment, and he was swept up again in the details of the
offensive.

During the night of July 17, the opposing Guard troops
quietly withdrew, and when dawn broke on the 18th, the trenches
opposite the FSLN battle line were empty. The planned attack was
hastily reorganized into a triumphal parade. Some 500 troops were
left behind to guard the FSLN positions, and the remaining 1,500
crammed into approximately 200 trucks, jeeps and hastily-
commandeered civilian vehicles to begin their victory procession
northward to Managua. The retreating Guard troops turned
toward the sea at La Virgen and swooped down on the small port
of San Juan del Sur where they seized tugboats, barges and fishing
vessels and fled up the coast toward El Salvador. The Benjamín
Zeledón column permitted them to escape and continued roaring
northward, because it was felt that the weight of their numbers
and their artillery might make a crucial difference in the
anticipated battle for Managua.

Ramón recalls:

We set off in an interminable file of jeeps and trucks toward
Managua. There were immense demonstrations of joy and
popular relief in every town we passed through. The entire
population was celebrating in the streets. They pressed food
and water on us, invited us into their houses for coffee. Our

reception in Managua was the same and even more so. I feel
that was the most important experience of our lives up to
that time.

There was no Battle of Managua. By the time the veterans of
the Southern Front arrived, Urcuyo the Brief had taken the last
plane for Guatemala, the Guard had laid down its arms and fled
in a pell-mell, every-man-for-himself scramble, and civil government had dissolved completely in the joyous effervescence of the
victory celebration. Ramón, Armando, and Santiago found each
other amidst the general disorder, and on the following day they
were among the hundreds of thousands who crammed the newly-
christened Plaza de la Revolución to welcome the governing Junta
that arrived in a triumphal cavalcade from León to begin the
arduous task of restoring order and consolidating the revolution
in Nicaragua.

CHAPTER 3

The 2 p.m. COPA flight from Panama landed on schedule at the newly renamed Augusto César Sandino airport of Managua, taxied to its parking circle and wheeled to a stop before the airport terminal. Three young women were among the first passengers to descend the gangway, stepping from the air-conditioned interior into the soggy, sauna bath heat of Nicaragua.

"Look, kids," Julia gestured with her chin at the huge banner stretched above the entrance doorway, "we've arrived in the Promised Land."

The banner read "Welcome to Free Nicaragua." Beneath it, a teenage *compa*, clad in an olive drab uniform several sizes too large for him and battered infantry boots, stood guard at the doorway. The FAL combat rifle slung over his shoulder was also too big for him.

It was only a few days after the triumph, and regular air traffic to and from Nicaragua had not yet been resumed. Consular offices all over Latin America and throughout Europe were closed as the Somoza regime's diplomats uneasily awaited instructions from the new authorities. Only a relative handful of passengers straggled behind the three women into the transit lounge; the remainder had read of the tumultuous disorder in Managua during this transitional period and cautiously preferred to remain aboard the plane during its brief pit-stop en route to Guatemala.

Susana's eyes swept the lounge appraisingly and fixed on a lanky *compa* guarding the doorway leading to the main lobby.

"That one," she decided. "Go get him, Julia, and make it good."

Julia was the right choice for this task. A tall, svelte brunette with chiseled features and green cat-eyes, she approached the guard and paralyzed him with a dazzling smile.

"Excuse me, *compañero*," she addressed him, "I must talk to the chief of Customs. It's most urgent."

The gawky youth's face lit up, and he managed:

"With pleasure, *señorita*. Just a moment."

As he turned, stuck his head through the door and shouted a name, Julia wheeled and beckoned to the other two. When the sentry turned back to face her, the three of them were standing shoulder to shoulder, and Julia announced regally, "They are with me."

Their escort was a petite *compita* with an Israeli Uzi machine pistol strapped over her shoulder. Her uniform was spotless, neatly pressed, and her boots were polished. Two heavy Indian braids hung down to her shoulders.

"Where did you fight?" Ana asked her as they crossed the lobby to the corridor at the far end.

"On the Rigoberto López Front," their guide replied. "I was in the assault on Asosasca Fortress and afterwards we came down through Nagarote and the new highway from León. It was heavy going, and we lost many *compas*."

She knocked on a door, waited for the response, and ushered them into a small office where a young man in rumpled olive drab removed his spectacles, rubbed his eyes wearily, replaced his glasses and arose to greet them. Julia went into action again.

"We're arriving from Spain," she told him. "We were held up in Caracas for several days because the airport here was closed during the takeover. We couldn't catch a flight to Guatemala until today. The important thing is that in the baggage compartment of the plane are three boxes of surgical instruments and antibiotics for the Military Hospital. We collected them through our Solidarity Committee in Barcelona, and we have to get them unloaded immediately before the plane takes off."

There was no further discussion, and within moments the three women and the overworked Customs officer were on the landing apron directing the unloading of the three boxes and their three suitcases. It wasn't until the baggage cart was safely inside the building that the young officer remembered to ask them for their travel documents. He held the three forged passports, Ana's handiwork, in his hands and cocked an eyebrow.

"Argentines?" he asked. "Where are your visas?"

"We're internationalist volunteers," Susana took charge for the first time. "We were exiled in Spain. Our *compañeros* have been fighting on the Southern Front. I'm sure Tomás Borge must know where we can find them."

The name had the anticipated effect. The Customs chief sighed. Everything was topsy turvy, and he would have felt infinitely more comfortable leading a guerrilla squad through the jungles of Nueva Segovia once again instead of struggling to bring order to the bureaucratic morass that had been handed him three days earlier. Besides, at that moment the jet engines of the COPA flight reverberated through the building as the plane wheeled sluggishly and headed for the end of the runway.

"There was no place to get visas," said Susana, judging the effect of her words, "and we had to buy passage for Guatemala in order to get off here and deliver these donated materials."

The Customs chief passed a palm across his forehead. He handed the three passports to the Immigration clerk and ordered:

"Give them entry visas for 30 days."

He shook hands with each of them.

"Welcome to Free Nicaragua," he said gravely, "and thank you for your contribution of international solidarity."

As he turned and strode back toward his offices, the three women exhaled with relief and collapsed on the mound of boxes and suitcases.

"We're here at last," Ana sighed, "but now, what on earth do we do?"

Susana recalls:

We were in the midst of another incredible adventure. Here we were at the Managua airport, and we didn't know where the others were. We had no idea where to go. Everything was unreal; it was like living a book by García Márquez. Macondo was Managua. We'd just come from Europe, and we couldn't comprehend anything. We were surrounded by all these kids as short as I am, heavily armed and sloppily dressed. The older ones had beards and looked as though they'd just come down from the mountains. The telephones didn't work and there was no public transport. We had no idea what we were going to do.

I remember that I wasn't well. A short time earlier I'd been treated for a stomach ulcer, and by the time we arrived I was feeling the effects of everything we'd been through: being delayed in Venezuela, the anxiety to get to Nicaragua. It had been a crazy kind of trip, and we were desperate to see the *compañeros* and learn whether or not they were all right. We had no idea where they were or if any of them had fallen in the fighting. All that was too much for me. Ana told me:

"Don't you move, Susana. Just sit here on your boxes."

I had brought the boxes in my name. I stayed there roosting on one box, surrounded by suitcases. The other two finally found a taxi and took off.

Julia and Ana asked the taxi driver where they would be most likely to find three Argentine *compas* who had fought on the Southern Front.

"All the foreigners live in the Las Colinas district," he assured them, and they drove off amidst the twisted girders and smoke-blackened wreckage of what had been Managua's industrial sector before Somoza's air force had bombed the area indiscriminately. The paving stone barricades defending the entrances to the eastern neighborhoods of the city were still standing. These octagonal concrete blocks, produced, ironically enough, by Somoza's own cement plant, formed the unbreachable walls that had held the Guard troops at bay during the seventeen days that the popular forces held out in Managua until their strategic withdrawal to Masaya.

The battered taxi dodged potholes in the streets forming the empty checkerboard of the *escombros*: what had been the center of Managua until the earthquake of 1972 and was now block after block of lush jungle undergrowth two meters tall.

Las Colinas, they discovered, was the residential area farthest from the airport, and the driver's suggestion, it was clear, had been motivated by greed rather than a desire to help. They circled aimlessly through the neighborhood, fruitlessly questioning occasional pedestrians, and finally ordered the driver to take them to the Intercontinental Hotel. Julia remembered reading in a recent newspaper that Tomás Borge had established his temporary headquarters there and might be able to help them in their search.

Borge's secretary had no idea where the three Argentine *compas* might be found, so Julia settled down forlornly in the lobby while Ana walked the few blocks uphill to the Military Hospital to inform authorities there of the three boxes of surgical equipment and medicine that were waiting at the airport, and to check the list of patients for familiar names.

Dusk was falling when the miracle occurred. Julia sprang up from her chair when the familiar, stocky figure entered the lobby.

"Gordo!" she cried. Armando turned to gape at her in disbelief and started firing questions as they flung their arms about each other:

"It's not true! When did you get here? How did you come?"

"We made it. It was awful; we were stuck in Caracas for three days after the triumph. Do you have a car?"

"Sure."

"Look, Ana is at the Military Hospital, and Susana is still at the airport with all the bags."

"Does Ramón know you're here?"

"Of course not. How could we get in touch?"

They picked Ana up first, and half an hour later they collected Susana and the baggage at the airport.

Susana recalls:

It was madness. We were whizzing through the *escombros* at 200 kilometers an hour with Armando at the wheel. I said:

"What's wrong, Gordo? Why are you going so fast? You'll kill us all."

"If I slow down, we'll be killed by the Guards hiding out there in the weeds."

"In that case, step on the gas," I told him.

We spread out, each of us to a different house. I accompanied Armando. After all, we have a history of being stuck with each other.

Susana's stomach pains eased, and that night she slept like a baby. The group was united again, the years of European exile ended.

CHAPTER 4

"That same afternoon, the 17th of July," Somoza laments in *Nicaragua Betrayed*, "I began making preparations to leave the United States."

> It seemed to me that Mr. Carter was going to turn me over to the Marxists of Nicaragua...That was a serious threat. If I were to be extradited, the least I could expect from the Marxist government of Nicaragua was a firing squad...I had been in the United States less than six hours. I sent Gen. Porras and an advance group to the Bahamas to make what arrangements they could for us to go there. After less than two days in the United States I was preparing to travel to Georgetown on Great Exuma island.
>
> The greater part of the government officials and military men who left Nicaragua on 17 July did so under the impression that one day they would return. Pezzullo had told me and members of my cabinet that we would not be away from Nicaragua for more than six months. All these people had left with the belief that a new government would soon be restructured and they would be able to return after a time...

The three women were in Caracas when they heard about Somoza's escape to the United States, and Susana recalls their reaction to the news:

> Yes, I remember. Since we were being delayed we were all together and we were mad. We were following the news hour by hour. When Somoza left, we were overjoyed, and at the same time we felt a great sadness because we hadn't arrived in time to take part in the fighting. On the one hand we were

happy that no more Nicaraguan blood would be shed, but we were frustrated at not having been able to fight side by side with the people. It took us a while to get over that.

By the time the three women arrived in Managua, Somoza had already departed Miami for temporary refuge in Great Exuma in the Caribbean and was putting out feelers to find out where his presence might be accepted by a host government on a permanent basis. The problem-strewn wanderings of the Shah of Iran following his deposition by the Muslim fundamentalists in February 1979 was very much on the minds of all government leaders at this time. United States acceptance of the Shah's presence for a delicate operation had resulted in threats and demands for his extradition by the new Iranian government and was to lead to the storming of the U.S. Embassy in Teheran and the holding of dozens of U.S. diplomats as hostages for more than a year. The Shah had already left the United States by the time Somoza's wanderings began and had been reluctantly granted refuge by Omar Torrijos in Panama as a personal favor to Jimmy Carter, who had pushed the Panama Canal Treaty through a reluctant Senate.

When we arrived in Nicaragua we realized that the war wasn't over. We remember those six months in 1979 that we spent in the country as a difficult time in which we had to fight, had to defend what had been won, had to undergo all the difficulties that were being experienced by the Nicaraguan people: shortages, counterrevolution, skirmishes. We participated in the defense and in the process of reconstruction, and we had the privilege of participation in the very beginnings of the revolution. Those first six months were an unforgettable period. I had to set aside all romantic notions and replace them with realism. Afterward, I regained the romanticism that is necessary and the love and sweetness, the idealism and sense of adventure that a revolutionary needs.

We were always soaking wet. We'd go out on night patrols in the rain with no lights, facing all sorts of problems. The difficulties we had with companions being wounded in confrontations were agonizing. Lots of times we went without food, without beds, without elemental medical assistance. It was a unique experience. The compañeros who went through that and maintained their willingness to do whatever the revolution needed—they were the best.

The new Nicaraguan government was able to draw on a wide range of top-level professional talent: economists, lawyers, university professors, engineers, agronomists, and even Catholic priests who had been open or secret sympathizers of the FSLN and staunch anti-Somocistas for years before the triumph. It was more difficult to fill the middle and lower levels of government with experienced people, and in the fields of public administration, education, and public health, for example, many teachers, nurses and public employees who had accepted the corruption of the Somoza regime without protest continued in their jobs. The problem of developing the police force and internal security, however, was most urgent. Public order had been nonexistent in Managua during the last weeks of the insurrection. Supermarkets and other commercial establishments had been ravaged by mobs of hungry people—and confirmed delinquents as well. The unoccupied homes of refugees who had fled the country were broken into and stripped. The *Mercado Oriental* was crammed with stolen goods, and the casual shopper could buy at ridiculously cut-rate prices everything from plumbing fixtures and electric fans to radios, television sets, deep freezers and air conditioners. The need to restore public order was accompanied by the equally urgent task of reducing the bands of armed former Guards who hid out in the *escombros* or in the warrens of the *Mercado Oriental* by day and who marauded by night to stay alive. All of these were hunted men who knew they faced a lengthy prison sentence if caught. They were prime fodder for the counter-revolution which was already being organized in rudimentary form. There was also another dissident ultra-leftist group, the *Milpas*, whose members had infiltrated the revolutionary militias and other FSLN structures. They were armed and harassed Managua at night by loosing random bursts of automatic weapons fire. In contradistinction to the Sandinista revolution, which proclaimed itself as anti-imperialist, democratic and popular, with a mixed economy and political pluralism, the *Milpa* slogan was: "The Sandinistas made the first revolution, but we'll make the second. All power to the workers and peasants."

More than anything else, during those first chaotic months until the Sandinista police and security forces could be organized and their members screened for loyalty, the revolution needed trustworthy, experienced personnel to restore public order and internal security.

Ramón explains:

> After the triumph of July 19, a number of commando squads were organized in each of the neighborhoods of Managua. They were organized in a rudimentary way without a centralized command at the national, or even the city level. They had the mission of controlling counterrevolutionary activities, and at the same time they dealt with typical police problems, such as robberies. They existed while the police force was being organized, as well as other organs of official legal control. Armando, Susana, and I participated in these commandos. Santiago stayed with his engineering battalion as an artillery officer.

Who, exactly, was this man, Ramón, who commanded the unwavering loyalty and confidence of a nucleus of Argentine revolutionaries to such a degree that they followed him into exile in Europe and then, at his behest, traveled to Nicaragua to take an active part in overthrowing the Somoza dictatorship and the self-sacrificing job of reestablishing public order and protecting the revolution's security at the lowest level by policing Managua's neighborhoods against common delinquents and roving, counter-revolutionary bands?

His true name is Enrique Haroldo Gorriarán Merlo, an Argentine of Basque origin, who at the time of these events was thirty-seven years old. His political career began in 1959 when he was a student and was inspired in great measure by the example of the Cuban revolution. Argentina had experienced continuing political instability since 1952. Every civilian government elected since that date had been overthrown by a military coup before it could complete its term in office. Ramón explained to us the origins of his political participation:

In the framework of that historical situation, that permanent political instability and constant dashing of the people's hopes, including my own, and encouraged by the example of the Cuban revolution, I started participating in the political struggle. I was studying economics at the time, and almost from the beginning I joined some compañeros who formed a part of the political organization that in 1964 became known as the Partido Revolucionario de los Trabajadores (Revolutionary Workers Party—PRT).

Gen. Onganía led another coup in 1966, establishing a repressive, anti-popular government that provoked increasing popular resistance, culminating in the "Cordobazo" of 1969, a mass mobilization in the center of the country that awakened increasingly violent echoes in other parts of the country during the following years. In 1970, the Fifth Congress of the PRT decided to create the Ejército Revolucionario del Pueblo (People's Revolutionary Army—ERP) as its action arm, and Ramón became one of its founders. Of the seven or eight politico-military organizations that sprang up at that time, the Peronist "Montoneros" and the socialist-oriented ERP were to achieve preeminence in the country, and Ramón became know nationally as one of the principal leaders until he was forced into exile following the Videla coup of 1976. Concerning his participation and that of his group in the Nicaraguan revolution, Ramón said:

We have always kept in mind that Latin America, during the epoch of the Spanish colonization as well as in the present phase of imperialism, has had the same enemy. The heroes of the first independence, among them San Martín and Bolivar, had a Latin-Americanist attitude. San Martín's soldiers shed their blood in Chile and Peru, and Bolivar's in

Colombia, Ecuador, and Venezuela. That is to say that the heroes of the first independence saw the Latin American revolution as one single thing. For them, each Latin American country that liberated itself from Spanish colonialism signified an advance in the revolutionary process that was developing in their own countries.

The first independence achieved political liberation, but the dominant classes of the epoch had no interest in a genuine independent development of our countries. Their economic dependence continued and deepened until imperialism, allied with our native oligarchies, was able to dominate Latin America. Colonial domination was replaced by the neo-colonial type.

Today our peoples have a single enemy, though of another nationality and another appearance. This new enemy has the same old objective: to exploit our labor and our natural resources. Because of this, the attitude of Bolivar, San Martín and the rest of the patriots who achieved the first independence, remains as valid today as it was yesterday. The Latin-Americanist attitude continued historically in Argentina. During the War of the Triple Alliance, the Montoneros under Chacho Peñaloza and Felipe Varela arose against Gen. Mitre, who as chief of the forces of Brazil, Uruguay and Argentina, was massacring the Paraguayan people.

We are partisans of this concept. For us, to help the Nicaraguan revolution was not only a matter of assisting a brother country, but it was also to help all the other liberation movements of Latin America in general and our own Argentina in particular. For us, there is no difference between fighting for the liberation of Nicaragua, El Salvador, or Argentina.

Ramón and the others were pleased with the contribution they had made and were making to the victory and consolidation of the revolution, but as the weeks and months passed and the new government became institutionalized, Ramón gradually grew more and more concerned that his small nucleus of ERP militants, once again honed to a finely-tempered edge, might become dispersed in the multiple tasks required by the revolution. He also felt that the group's presence in Nicaragua was no longer as important as it had been at the beginning.

The three of them, Ramón, Santiago, and Armando, had formed the habit of meeting once a week at *El Gaucho* restaurant to share various pitchers of beer and savor a barbecued meal. It wasn't up to Argentine standards, they agreed, with *chinchulines*, *molleja* and all the trimmings. Nevertheless, Nicaraguan beef was excellent, and the method of preparation, roasting it slowly over charcoal embers, was familiar enough to arouse their nostalgia for the *Río de la Plata*.

On that particular afternoon, Ramón brought up the worrisome situation in Argentina and the other problem that preoccupied him: the need to preserve the cohesion of the little group of veterans who were presently in Nicaragua.

"It seems to me we have quite a wait ahead of us before we can return," he told them. "We're faced with a necessary transition period during which we don't want to lose our primary identity as Argentine revolutionaries."

Santiago and Armando agreed.

"Since we can't return immediately, we should start thinking about carrying out some activities that tie us more closely to the Argentine and Latin American revolutionary process."

"There's no question about that," Santiago nodded. "And it should be something that strengthens the bonds between us and the *compañeros* who are still inside Argentina. Once again, we're at the stage of accumulating forces."

Ramón switched the conversation to the increasing evidence of a structured counterrevolutionary movement outside Nicaragua, whose principal assets were the bands of former Somoza Guards along the Honduran border.

Somebody was holding them there, he observed, in provisional encampments, but with military discipline and with adequate provisions of food and ammunition for the arms they had brought with them. Somebody was holding them there, spurring them to make periodic irruption's into Nicaraguan territory to attack isolated farms, assassinate the inhabitants and drive the livestock back across the border to provide their meat supply.

Then too, Somoza was making frequent boastful statements in interviews about his plans to return triumphantly to Nicaragua once his archenemy, Jimmy Carter, was out of the presidency. It became clear from newspaper accounts that the funds to sustain these paramilitary bands of cattle rustlers were coming from Miami. Somoza obviously was investing some of his ill-gotten fortune in supporting the potential army of the counter-revolution. Ramón had no doubt that the CIA would soon take over the bulk of that funding, if it hadn't already done so, but still, Somoza, even in exile, was the front man for the forces of U.S. and Nicaraguan reaction, just as he was the agglutinating factor for the contras: the individual to whom the former Guard officers were personally loyal and the only man they could look to in the hope that they might return and lord over the nation as they and their predecessors had grown accustomed to doing for the past fifty years.

"It makes me furious to think of that criminal enjoying his millions far away in Paraguay," Armando huffed, "while he still controls the strings to try to destroy this revolution."

"You'll have to give him credit for finding the right place to hide," Santiago offered. "I read somewhere that Samuel Genie has at least twelve security guards watching over him day and night, not to mention Stroessner's police and security forces. I don't doubt that he's found himself a fortress like the Tiscapa bunker to live in."

Ramón watched them attentively, weighing their words before interjecting himself into the conversation again.

"Still, he must be worried," he mused. "According to the newspapers, he hardly ever lets himself be seen. He never frequents night clubs or places like that."

"In Asunción there are no night clubs," Armando snorted. "It's a hick town if I ever saw one."

"A quiet place," Ramón shrugged. "Just what he needs for his bad heart. He'll probably die of cirrhosis at age eighty-five."

"Ah no!" Armando exclaimed, "It would be a historic disgrace to permit that murderer to die peacefully in bed."

"Armando is right," Santiago chimed in. "Somebody ought to wipe him off the face of the earth."

"Very well, *compañeros*..." Ramón paused to give more weight to what he was about to say. "In that case, why don't we have a go at it?"

CHAPTER 5

Ramón chuckled at the startled expressions on his listeners' faces.

"Well, why not?" he asked. He nodded toward Santiago, whose eyes had narrowed thoughtfully as he digested the idea.

"Go ahead, Flaco," he coaxed. "You be the devil's advocate and tell us why we can't do it."

Santiago started speaking in a quiet voice, as if thinking out loud.

"In the first place, now that the Somozas are gone, Stroessner's dictatorship is the oldest in Latin America. He's been in power for, let's see, twenty-five years now, and there's not a whisper of opposition in the country. He's managed to do what the Somozas couldn't, even by murdering Sandino: he's managed to decapitate the revolutionary opposition and stamp out each new sprout that emerges. He has achieved a historic cut-off, which means he has a deadly, efficient security service and informers all over the place. We'd have to slip past them even before getting close to Samuel Genie, Somoza's old security chief, and his gang of thugs..."

"Or maybe, we'll discover that Stroessner's security people have grown sloppy and overconfident because they've had no serious opposition to contend with for so long a time."

"I wouldn't bet on that," Armando broke in. "Remember back in '72 after we recuperated all those arms from the 141st Battalion in Cordoba and some Paraguayan *compas* talked us into smuggling a consignment across the river? We never heard of the arms again, nor of the *compas* either. The *pampa* swallowed them, and there wasn't even a mention of it in the newspapers. Now that's what I call efficiency."

"All right," Ramón nodded, "let's leave that question open until we have more facts. What's your next point, Flaco?"

"An extension of the earlier one," Santiago continued. "We'd have to move into unexplored territory, a mine field of unknown dangers, without being able to count on any support infrastructure already in place. We'd have to improvise everything on the spot in a hostile environment—safe houses, security procedures, transport, smuggling in weapons, surveillance of Somoza's movements. We'd have to start the whole thing from scratch. On top of all that, we're foreigners—Argentines. Strangers in a strange land."

"There are hundreds of Argentines crossing the river every day to take advantage of the black market," Ramón countered. "We could lose ourselves in all that movement. Just think of the problems a Central American team would have in taking on a job like this. They'd be spotted in a minute. I would bet there's been a tail on every Central American in Asunción since Somoza arrived there. We'd have an easier time of it."

"Besides that," Armando snorted, "the Sandinistas are trying to do it legally; they're trying to extradite him and bring him back here to stand trial, for Chris' sake. That must give Somoza a laugh. Stroessner has been protecting Nazi war criminals and international dope dealers for the past twenty years, and getting rich in the process."

"I don't claim it will be easy," Ramón took the floor, "but let's take a look at the other side. It would be expensive, but that's why we have the Swiss bank account. We'd need weapons, but we still have some stashed away in Argentina that we took away from the 141st. And the river is a smuggler's paradise. As you pointed out, Gordo, we've already run guns across there, and most important, we have collaborators inside Argentina to help us."

"Hmm." Santiago was dubious. "We couldn't go in cold and stumble our way through an operation like that. We'd have to pick our people carefully and train them for every single contingency we might run into."

"I know," Ramón nodded. "We'll have to set up a training program and decide what kind of a team we need, and how many.

I'm handing you that assignment, Flaco. But we're getting ahead of ourselves. First of all, do either of you have any objections to taking on this job? Any moral qualms, let's say?"

Santiago shook his head definitively.

"We'd be doing a favor to humanity," Armando erupted. "We've all seen the horrors Somoza committed here: the mass graves, the young men in the street with both hands chopped off, the thousands of innocents he killed with indiscriminate bombardments. For my part, I think that all these tinhorn dictatorships should be taught that revolutionary justice never sleeps and they can no longer get away with their crimes and then leave the country to settle down peacefully with their stolen riches and their bodyguards."

"We'd be doing a great favor to the Nicaraguan revolution," Santiago mused.

"And not only that," Ramón added, "but it would be a crushing demonstration of Latin Americanist solidarity that would send chills down the backs of the Pinochets, Videlas and the faceless generals of Uruguay, not to mention Stroessner and the rotating dictators here in Central America.

"Another thing: while we were helpful here, we were never indispensable to the Nicaraguan revolution, and that is even truer today. I think the best way we can help the revolution is to carry out the job we are talking about. Furthermore, I think we have to return to our own path for the sake of all the *compañeros* who fell in Argentina and didn't live to see our revolution triumph. What do you think?"

Santiago nodded.

"We've also agreed that it's still premature to return to our own country. We have *compañeros* there who are capable of keeping the revolutionary spark alive, and they have the advantage of legal status. We'd be more of a hindrance than a help right now. This gives us enough time to make sure that Somoza gets what he has coming, and it doesn't interfere with our final objective. Do you agree?"

The other two nodded, and Armando asked, "Do you think we should tell the Sandinistas what we have in mind?"

"Not a word!" Ramón cut him short. "The mere fact of telling them would compromise them. They aren't a guerrilla movement any longer; they're running a state, and for reasons of state I'm certain they wouldn't approve. Later, if we're successful and live to tell about it, we can let them know. But right now, we can't say a word about this even to the other members of our group."

"Sooner or later the others will have to know," Armando ventured.

"That moment will come," Ramón assured him, "but only for those who are involved in the project. And before that happens, we have a lot of work ahead of us. You, Armando, should start collecting all available information about Somoza's activities in Asunción: where he lives, what business activities he's involved in, what circles he moves in, how many people besides Genie are in his bodyguard, whether or not his limousine is bulletproof, etceteras. We're starting from square one, and any crumb of information may prove useful."

Armando was visibly content to be assigned a concrete task.

"We'll have to work out various operational plans and calculate the number of people required for different scenarios," Ramón continued. "We'll also have to make arrangements for a future delivery of arms. But above all, we'll have to figure out how an exiled dictator is predisposed to behave. Here is a person who still has a political objective in mind and enormous economic resources, a man who has been the center of reactionary politics in Central America for years. How does his mind work these days?"

Armando, Santiago, and Ramón set about their various tasks and kept on lunching at "El Gaucho" restaurant once a week to keep each other informed of their progress.

Armando started by visiting the two daily newspapers in Managua and going through all issues for the past three months in search of references to Somoza's wanderings and his settling down in Asunción. The results were, for the most part, disappointing. He had more luck when he extended his search to the periodicals section of the two university libraries and the reading room of the Ministry of Foreign Affairs. After several weeks of effort, however, he came to the conclusion that almost all of the vital information the team required would have to be gathered by on-the-spot observation, surveillance and legwork in Asunción itself.

When Santiago had the night-watch at the engineering battalion's command post, he kept a small notebook before him which he had inaugurated with three numbered commandments:

I. Enter without arousing suspicion.

II. Do the job without getting caught.

III. Get away without leaving a trace.

Classical simplicity itself, he thought, as he reread the points that first night. All we have to teach them is how to create and document a false identity and then to live that identity without slip-ups for X period of time while zeroing in on the target without attracting the attention of national security police, local police, Somoza's bodyguards, and nosy neighbors. Then, how to set an infallible trap, bring in the arms and other technical equipment needed to accomplish the job, use it swiftly and efficiently at the proper moment, gather up everything without leaving behind a single scrap of evidence, and disappear smoothly and silently along a prearranged escape route. During the course of the operation, team members would have to know how to arrange clandestine meetings or dead-drops for passing along information and instructions, how to detect surveillance and shake it off without arousing the shadower's suspicions, how to live their cover convincingly and move with transparent anonymity through an unfamiliar city for an indeterminate period of time.

Child's play, he thought with a grin. It shouldn't call for more than a three-month course of eight-hour days for classroom work and field practice, with no days off. He bent over the notebook and started elaborating each mental note in a small, precise, school-teacher's script.

Ramón whistled tunelessly as he folded and smoothed a bed sheet into an improvised ironing pad atop the kitchen table. He licked a forefinger and tapped it against the face of the iron. It spat back at him. Next, he removed a clean handkerchief from his pocket, held it under the running tap for a few seconds and then wrung it nearly dry. Lastly, he took the clean sheet of typing paper from his desk in the next room, placed it on the ironing pad, covered it with the damp handkerchief and ran the hot iron over it, first up and down and then crosswise several times until the handkerchief was smooth and dry. He unplugged the iron, removed the handkerchief and held the sheet of paper up to the light. It was pristine, virginal. He turned it edgewise to the light and scanned its innocent surface. Perfect.

Out of long habit, he removed the evidence of his recent activity, folding the handkerchief and returning it to his pocket, returning the sheet to the linen closet, placing the electric iron on the metal sink top to cool. He sat down at the desk, rolled the sheet into the portable typewriter and started typing:

San José, Costa Rica
28 October 1979

Dear Mario:

I hope this finds you and your family in good health.
Here, the business is limping along more or less, but I
sometimes ask myself: how in the world did it occur to
me to open a *gaucho* restaurant in a country where
international tourist traffic is almost nonexistent...

The sheet of paper contained another, invisible message for Mario. Did he, it inquired, happen to have in stock such items as:
   2 automatic assault rifles, one with sniper scope,
   2 Browning 9 mm. pistols,
   2 Ingram submachine guns with silencers,
   1 RPG-7 bazooka with two projectiles,
   4 fragmentation grenades?
   If so, the secret message continued, please make sure they are in good working order; be prepared to pack them and accom-

panying ammunition for shipment and stand by for further instructions.

Ramón had written other letters concerning another topic to *compañeros* of the ERP in Venezuela, Colombia, and Peru during recent days, and now, while awaiting replies, he could turn his attention to refining the training program with Santiago and devote more thought to selecting the members of the future commando team.

CHAPTER 6

The New Year's Eve party to usher in 1980 was an unqualified success. El Gordo, who enjoyed cooking almost as much as he enjoyed eating, took charge of the Argentine style *asado* while Susana acted as barmaid. Someone commented that this was the first time they'd all gotten together in the same room since their arrival in Managua, and the ten of them raised their glasses and drank to that. Ramón, sitting in the Masayan rocking chair at the edge of the group, permitted himself a tight smile. He'd seen to that. The *asado* was done to perfection, Julia's tossed salad with Chontales cheese dressing was just the right complement, and everybody, having indulged a bit too much in Nicaragua Libres (Flor de Caña Extra Dry Rum on the rocks with half a squeezed lime), fell silent as they downed the food.

Afterwards, El Flaco got the party going by turning up the record player and dancing a *mambo* solo.

"La guitarra, la guitarra!" the crowd chorused, and Santiago picked up the instrument, plucked out the opening chords of *Mi Buenos Aires Querido* and got them all singing old favorites: tangos, *zambas*, *milongas* and *chacareras*. Nostalgia for the distant homeland invaded each of them. El Flaco recalled the dusty streets of his Santiago del Estero and the aridity of that landscape that contrasted so strongly with the green of Managua after the winter rains. Ramón summoned up a vision of the banks of the Paraná and the home of his parents, which he hadn't visited for years.

The first thing anyone knew it was midnight, and the din of firecrackers and rockets going off all over town reminded half of those present of the battles on the *Frente Sur*.

Ramón arose and offered a toast to the Sandinista revolution and then another to an early return to their Argentine homeland.

"Very well, *compañeros*," he continued as they all lowered their glasses. "As I think I've told each of you separately, it's time to get back to work before we all wind up like Armando here."

Armando's features reddened, and he tucked his head down over the charred rib bone he was furtively gnawing.

"I wanted us to get together to celebrate the end of this eventful year and to propose to all of you a preparatory phase before returning to the country," Ramón went on. "Many of us have been away for a number of years, and we've no doubt forgotten many of the practical skills we had to learn the hard way. For that reason, Santiago and I are preparing an intensive training program that should bring all of us back to a state of readiness. Within a week, more or less, we'll start moving out in small groups to Bogotá. We have a training site awaiting us, not too far from the capital, and the course will begin on the 15th. During the next two or three months we'll get to know each other better than ever and, just as important, we'll all learn a great deal about our own strengths and weaknesses."

Everyone present had received a hint, usually from Ramón himself, that something was in the wind and that they should be making preparations to leave. Finally, the new project was out in the open and they could all talk about it. The news obviously called for another drink.

"Colombia was a country that offered favorable conditions," Ramón explained to us. "Argentine citizens don't need entry visas, and the length of stay for tourists is three months renewable for another three-month period. Bogotá is a big city that permits maneuverability without serious problems."

The training site was a country house approximately two hours south of Bogotá. It was surrounded by almost two acres of orchard, and all the "students" could squeeze into the house with a bit of crowding. There were other houses in the vicinity, but none of them was visible.

During the first weeks of January as the team members began arriving in ones and twos, the internal administration of their residential school began to function. Each individual took turns cooking, washing dishes, cleaning, and standing sentry duty day and night. Despite the fact that the house was isolated from the nearest neighbors, a strict rule was established from the outset: during daylight hours no more than three persons at a time could be visible outside the house so as not to arouse the suspicions of an unexpected visitor.

A Colombian married couple who were concerned with Latin American problems helped us out by renting the house in advance, Ramón told us. Naturally, they had no notion of our real motives. They were elderly people with whom we had gotten acquainted in mid-1977, and they only knew we were revolutionaries who were persecuted in Argentina. Once in a while, on weekends, they would come to visit us.

The group also had the friendly collaboration of a sister revolutionary organization in Colombia. This group counseled them as to precautions to be taken when moving about in Bogotá and, more importantly, made available the arms required for their military training: two .22 carbines with telescopic sights, two 9 mm. automatics, two M-16 assault rifles, one FAL combat rifle, two l9 mm. submachine guns plus explosives and slow fuses.

"They thought we were setting up a training course for *compañeros* who were to return to Argentina," Ramón explained, "and we never spoke of our real objective."

The real objective was held secret from the trainees themselves because Ramón and Santiago still did not know who would be selected for the commando unit. Nevertheless, as the first weeks went by, some members of the group began to suspect that a large-scale special operation was in the works. The course of studies itself gave away the fact that this was not a kindergarten course in general clandestine techniques.

The day began with rigorous calisthenics followed by a martial arts course taught by Santiago. This compensated in part for the sedentary routine observed during the rest of the day when the students were cooped up in the house to concentrate on theoretical studies. They soon realized that Santiago's schooling was sharpening their muscle tone and that he was observing them with an eagle eye to detect any lack of agility or muscular coordination. Most of them shed several kilos because of this strenuous physical training.

Ramón took charge of their theoretical training in conspiratorial techniques and typical methods employed by intelligence and state security services in Southern Cone countries. Ana assisted him with a course on falsification of documents and the normal procedures used by immigration and customs police in different countries.

One of the courses dealt with clandestine communication techniques: codes and ciphers, secret writing, the selection of dead drops for depositing and recovering messages. Still another concerned the fabrication of cover stories for any occasion and the need for not carrying anything on one's person that contradicted that cover. It also included techniques for changing one's appearance, basic techniques for moving about without calling attention to oneself, how to choose sites for clandestine meetings, as well as how to pass written messages without being noticed.

There was even a course in surveillance and counter-surveillance that seemed more like a child's game. This offered the group a chance to vary the claustrophobic routine and spend a day in Bogotá once in a while. The game consisted of the following: two persons worked out plans for a clandestine rendezvous in a certain part of the city, setting off from departure points known to all the participants. The other members of the group had to follow them without being discovered and observe all their movements: detecting whether they deposited or received a written message, whether they communicated or met with the other party, etc. Armando, who relished the game more than anyone else, won the competition easily by disguising himself in a peasant's straw hat and sandals and renting an ice cream wagon, at an exorbitant price, from its dumbfounded owner. He crossed the departure line jingling his bell without being recognized by the others and tranquilly accomplished his mission. Half an hour later he returned, doffed his hat and presented each of his befuddled pursuers with a popsicle. He also insisted on taking them all to lunch at a tempting seafood restaurant he had discovered during his morning stroll.

Each of the team members became expert at handling the various weapons they had at their disposal, learning to disassemble and assemble them blindfolded. They had to drive for an hour to an uninhabited spot in the mountains for target practice so that the noise of small arms fire would not arouse suspicions.

Susana recalls:

I had very little military experience, and had hardly ever fired a gun. One time we were engaged in target practice there in the mountains. Santiago was behind me, and I had to fire an M-16 from a kneeling position. Something was wrong with the ammunition, and when I pulled the trigger the cartridge blew up in the chamber. I dropped the rifle instinctively. I was deafened and my cheek was burning. The weapon was red hot and smoking, and the cartridge chamber was ruined.

Santiago grabbed me from behind and lifted me to my feet. He wrapped his arms around me, gave me a big bear hug and told me everything was all right. I was scared stiff, but I got over it quickly because Santiago had done exactly the right thing at the right time, and I wasn't traumatized by the experience.

Santiago was a serene, tranquil person. He had one fundamental attitude toward the rest of us: he was a teacher; he was teaching us all the time. He had spent a great part of his militant life giving political and military classes. He also transmitted a sense of complete security and self-assurance. I had known him since 1973 when we worked together in the province of Cordoba. Santiago was already famous then; he was "Captain Santiago."

Captain Santiago was a legend in Argentine revolutionary circles, and also in the enemy ranks. Together with Ramón, he had participated in the creation of the People's Revolutionary (ERP) and from the beginning had proved himself to be an intrepid military leader. When Communications Battalion 141 surrendered its arms to the ERP in Cordoba, Santiago led one of the combat groups and was subsequently decorated with the Order *Heroes of Trelew*, a medal awarded by the ERP for heroic actions.

Hugo Irarzún, his true name, was designated at that time a member of the Central Committee of the Party in military functions. One of his first combat actions following that promotion was the one in which the Blue Armored Regiment operation won him a second Heroes of Trelew medal. All by himself, using a FAL combat rifle with grenade launcher, he kept an entire company immobilized for more than an hour, after which he withdrew unscathed from the field of battle.

According to Osvaldo, another ERP militant in the Cordoba Regiment:

> He was very cool in combat, and besides that a born teacher with a solid political and ideological foundation. He wasn't limited to being a military instructor. Lots of us still remember the rigorousness of his courses in philosophy, Argentine history, and economics in the PRT's political training school. Whenever the going was rough, the warmth and affection of his presence gave us a sense of security.

Under Santiago's direction, the students learned to prepare and detonate explosive charges, and they developed into expert sharpshooters with both open and telescopic sights. They all learned how to handle a bazooka, using a homemade 3-inch plastic plumbing tube as a model, and they were drilled constantly in the basic military tactics of small units: how to take advantage of natural cover, how to lay down covering fire to protect a temporarily-exposed comrade, how to crawl and roll without clogging one's weapon, and all the other immemorial infantry tricks.

Armando recalls the training period as "a lovely time":

> The important thing was that we systematized all our previous knowledge. Most of us had quite a bit of practical experience, but I, for one, had never had any systematic military training. It helps a lot. It taught me that the things I had learned empirically are much more effective when you apply scientific methods to them. We got to know each other intimately and were able to recognize each other's defects

and virtues. Despite the fact that we were confined together in close quarters, we never had any interpersonal friction. Instead, we went through a period of solidifying our relations with each other and with the group as a whole.

Ramón had also seen to it that the group did not lack reading material in their relatively few hours of leisure. He had thoughtfully provided the improvised school with a small but select library featuring such titles as: *The Red Orchestra, The Spy Who Came in from the Cold, The Day of the Jackal,* and *The House on Garibaldi Street* which dealt with the operation against Eichmann on the part of the Israeli intelligence service.

The course lasted longer than either Ramón or Santiago had originally anticipated. Ramón had long since made his selection of the individuals who were to make up the commando team, but none of them as yet had any hint of what lay ahead. In April, Ramón decided that the time had come to send out an advance scouting party.

Morning exercises and breakfast were behind them, and as the others settled down in the living room for a lecture by Santiago, Ramón stepped into the kitchen where Susana and Francisco were finishing the morning cleanup duties.

"Let's go for a walk," he suggested, and the three of them left the house by the kitchen door and strolled out beyond the neatly-tended vegetable garden to settle down beneath a large shade tree at the far end of the property.

There he broke the news to them: Anastasio Somoza Debayle was the target of their forthcoming operation, and the two of them were to be the first to enter Paraguay and gather the basic information without which concrete operational planning could not go forward.

Susana smiled in recollection:

I have to confess that I was terribly naive up to the last minute. I suppose it's a question of conspiratorial methods. One simply learns not to speculate about things one isn't told. Not until the day that Ramón sat me down with Francisco and proposed that we travel to Paraguay to undertake the initial reconnaissance did I realize that we were involved in an operation. My greatest ambition was to return to Argentina, and I thought we were simply systematizing our knowledge so we could go back and live clandestinely as we had before, and continue the revolutionary struggle, taking into account the changes that had taken place during our absence.

I'll admit that the idea of the operation stunned me; at the beginning it seemed simply incredible. I began to realize that everything we had preached for years, international solidarity, was also involved here. It wasn't only a continuation of what we had already done, of coming to help Nicaragua win its struggle and to participate in the first phase of the revolutionary process, but it was going a step further, because internationalism was not merely a matter of helping Nicaragua but also of helping the entire continent by seeing to it that a monster like Somoza didn't escape justice with impunity. We all felt defrauded that the crimes of Batista and other tyrants had remained unpunished. It needed to be reversed. The continent needed it; the peoples of Latin America required it; the revolutionaries and all the thousands of fallen martyrs demanded it.

It was a way of carrying out a definitive act of justice, just as Rigoberto López Pérez had done with Somoza's father. It was time to put an end to the unwritten law that "dictators get off scot-free." I understood the need for this. Besides that, I was fascinated by the operational problem and delighted to have the privilege of participating in the project—because it was a privilege to participate, together with my *compañeros*, in a concrete, objective action that dovetailed directly with the Nicaraguan and the continental revolutionary movements.

I was taught, along with the other compañeros, that revolutions are not only national, but also continental and international movements. Che taught us that with the concrete example of his entire life. He died fighting and preaching the need for Latin American unity. He taught us that when democratic forms of expression do not exist, armed struggle is the only valid response to dictatorship. That might have been questioned immediately after he fell in combat, but not any longer because the Nicaraguan revolution demonstrated it once again in practice, and the Salvadoran revolution is in the process of demonstrating it. The revolutionaries in Guatemala and all through the rest of the continent are perfectly clear that when people are denied free political expression, armed struggle is the only valid answer. Moreover, this has been demonstrated by existing revolutions, not just in theoretical treatises. We have one revolution with twenty-five years of existence, another with five and a third that is in the making. The Salvadorans are in the midst of the process, and I'm confident that they'll be successful.

All these things flashed through my mind while Ramón was talking to us, and they filled me with, I don't know how to explain it, with enthusiasm, optimism, and determination.

CHAPTER 7

Susana's and Francisco's first stop was in Río de Janeiro where they registered at a modest hotel in the center of town, well away from the luxury hotel strip of Copacabana. They were a honeymooning couple making the grand tour of South America, in case anyone asked, but nobody did. Particularly not in the periodicals room of the public library where they spent two days searching through back issues of Brazilian, Argentine, and Paraguayan newspapers and magazines for any mention of Somoza's activities since his arrival in Paraguay.

Their first morning's search left them both elated. Newspaper accounts gave them the information that Somoza lived on the Avenida Mariscal López in Asunción and that, when he appeared in the city, his chauffeured limousine was invariably accompanied by a red Ford Falcon carrying four bodyguards. Other accounts speculated that he might be considering extensive real estate investments in Paraguay. The two of them celebrated by taking the cable car to the top of Sugar Loaf and, after enjoying the unequaled view, having lunch in the tourist restaurant perched atop the gray stone dome. On their way back to the library, Francisco stopped at a travel agency to make reservations for the flight to Asunción two days later, double-checked to make sure that Argentine citizens did not require visas nor vaccination certificates in order to enter the country, and picked up a tourist brochure giving the schedule of all international flights between Brazil and Paraguay.

They gleaned little additional information during their next day at the library, save for a few gossip items about Somoza and his mistress, Dinorah Sampson, from women's magazines. During their last night in Río, Susana wrote a condensed report of their findings in a chatty letter to Ramón in which Somoza was referred to as "Eduardo," a name they had chosen in advance. She included the flight schedule in her letter and mailed it to Ramón's postal box in Bogotá the next morning as they checked out of the hotel bound for the airport.

The two of them had memorized a lengthy list of Ramón's instructions and information before leaving Colombia, and a good many of these had to do with immigration and customs procedures and security measures in force at the Asunción airport. On arrival, they straggled behind other disembarking passengers while filling out their tourist cards and were the last in line at the immigration booth. The immigration officer glanced at their falsified passports and flipped through the pages to find the first available blank space on which to stamp the entry seal. Customs inspection was also a cursory spot-check. Francisco's bag was opened and halfheartedly pawed through; Susana's was not. It was, they agreed, the normal routine for international airports. There were several uniformed airport guards in the lobby, and Francisco thought he detected several plain-clothes security guards loitering at the exit from the immigration stand, but you couldn't really tell.

On the way out to the taxi stand, Francisco picked up a list of hotels and two maps of the city at the Tourist Information booth. The horizon was flat in all directions as they drove toward the city—desolate pampas, punctuated only by monotonous thorn trees. Asunción, they soon discovered, was not a great deal better—a somnolent river town with an unimpressive commercial district.

"It looks as though it went into suspended animation a quarter of a century ago," Susana murmured to Francisco so that the taxi driver would not overhear.

"It did," Francisco grinned back at her. "That's when Stroessner took over."

Their hotel was unimpressive, fair-to-middling clean, and their room had that anonymous, down-at-the-heel unpresumptuousness that second-class hotel rooms have all over the world. They bought all the newspapers they could find at a street corner kiosk after a cursory stroll through the center of town.

Susana shook her head and remarked, "I have the feeling that after we've been here for two weeks we'll know everyone in town by sight."

"Think small," Francisco advised her, "think invisible. Just don't start dancing in the streets."

It was even difficult to locate a passable restaurant that evening, but they finally settled for a Swiss restaurant half a block away from the main thoroughfare, and Susana chuckled, as they took their seats at a table, that this paucity was going to make Armando very unhappy.

Early the next morning, Susana and Francisco took a cab to the Avenida Mariscal López to carry out the first—and most important—of their assignments: to locate Somoza's residence and discover what kind of security precautions Samuel Genie had surrounded the ex-dictator with. The two of them had studied the city map with care over their breakfast coffee.

When they turned into the wide residential avenue, Susana asked the cab driver casually, "They've told us that former President Somoza lives around here. Is that true?"

"Yes," their driver replied. "His house is just down the street. It's always surrounded by a bunch of policemen. I'll point it out to you."

The driver slowed some two blocks farther along the avenue and pointed to a house ahead of them across the street.

"That's Somoza's residence," he said, "but it's very strange; there are no guards around."

As they cruised past, they saw that the house was obviously uninhabited, and there was a cardboard sign tacked to the walled entrance portal that stated in large block letters: "For Rent."

Susana and Francisco stared at each other, speechless.

"Well," the driver shrugged, "he was still here three weeks ago. He must have moved very recently."

They paid off the taxi several blocks further along the street and, crestfallen, walked back past the erstwhile residence. Susana memorized the telephone number of the real estate agency on the rental sign and, a few steps further on, they confronted a young Paraguayan mother wheeling a baby carriage.

"Is it true that former President Somoza doesn't live here any longer?"

"Yes," she responded, "he moved away a few weeks ago."

"Do you know where he lives now?"

"I haven't the faintest idea."

Nobody seemed to know where the former dictator had taken up residence. The couple adopted their honeymooners' air and caught another cab for a sightseeing tour of the city. The driver pointed out various public buildings and took them past Stroessner's presidential residence, but when they asked to see where Somoza lived, he took them back to Avenida Mariscal López and was as surprised as the first had been to see the "For Rent" sign at the entrance.

They returned to the hotel, and Susana telephoned the rental agency. She was, she explained, the representative of a furniture company in Buenos Aires and Dinorah Sampson had written some weeks previously concerning the redecoration of her new living room. Could the agency provide the new address of the Somoza entourage?

The answer was no, the agency could not. Click.

By now they had acquired a general familiarity with the contours of the best residential areas of Asunción, and Francisco had rented a car. They already knew that Somoza had purchased an elegant home on the shores of Lake Ipacari, and they set out for the lake with high expectations. They rented a rickety motor launch, and the boatman willingly pointed out President Stroessner's lakeside residence and the nearby Somoza residence as well, but he explained that it was a secured area and boats were forbidden to approach that part of the lake, even when neither family was in residence, as was now the case. Somoza and Dinorah, he added, had hardly ever visited the lake except during the first few weeks they owned the house.

After their boating expedition, Susana sketched a map showing the location of the two houses with respect to the public bathing area, and they set off in the car to drive past the two houses from the shore side. The only possible entrance by car was blocked with a heavy chain, and they both agreed it would be foolhardy as well as pointless to enter the area on foot and risk being stopped by resident security guards.

Back in Asunción, Francisco even resorted to the unlikely ruse of visiting pharmacies near the residential zone to buy a vial of digitalis and confide jokingly to the attendants that he suffered the same ailment as former president Somoza, whom he understood lived somewhere nearby. His stratagem was a total failure.

"There must be an easier way," Susana brooded as they sat down for lunch on their third day of fruitless searching. As they ate silently, the glimmerings of an idea stirred in Susana's mind, and over coffee she told Francisco: "I'm going directly to his house today." She outlined her scheme to him, and he agreed it was certainly worth a try. The two of them checked the proposal step-by-step, to be certain that she would not leave a trail or arouse undue suspicions.

Susana told us:

That afternoon I dressed with a certain discreet elegance, and Francisco dropped me off near the Hotel Guaraní and waited for me at a nearby cafe. The Guaraní is in the center of town. It's a meeting place for the upper class, the richest people, diplomats, the CIA, etc. There's always a line of taxis at the main entrance, and most of the drivers are police informers. I walked into the hotel, went to the ladies' room where I painted my eyes and mouth high society style and fixed my hair differently. Next, I went to the cafeteria, had a cup of tea and walked out as if I were a hotel guest.

I climbed into a taxi and told the driver, "A friend of mine has recommended a beauty parlor to me, but she couldn't explain how to get there. It's the same parlor Dinorah Sampson uses, and it's three blocks down from General Somoza's residence and one block to the left."

The taxi driver was very amiable, and first he asked the other drivers in the queue. Nobody knew. Next he went into a lottery agency. He spoke to the owner in Guaraní. I didn't understand what he was saying, but I heard the word 'Somoza' and I knew he was trying. He returned to the cab disconsolately and told me in Spanish that the man had moved recently and nobody knew where his new house was located.

He didn't want to lose the trip, because the fare was adding up, and besides I told him, "If you find me that beauty parlor, you'll have a good tip coming."

"Don't worry," he told me, "I'll find it for you."

We turned up Avenida España near the center of town, and he stopped at a police station along the way. He got out and asked me to wait while he checked. I kept an eye on him, a bit nervous about what might happen. In a few minutes he returned and told me, "They said it's not too far from here, and it's located along this very avenue."

All the while we'd been chatting. He asked me what I worked at, and I told him I worked for UNESCO and that's why I traveled so much.

We were looking for the beauty parlor now, and I saw that he was slowing down and looking at the houses, so I asked him, "Which is the Somoza residence?"

"It's one of these," he said, "so from here I have to go three blocks further."

I wasn't clear as to which house it was, and I wanted to know precisely. We went ahead slowly, and at the end of three blocks he stopped, looked and said: "No, this is a dead-end street."

"Go another block," I told him.

We went to the corner, turned left, and I couldn't believe my eyes! There was a beauty parlor in the middle of the block. We were in an expensive residential zone with nothing but mansions and blocks and blocks of houses. It was a very high-class beauty parlor.

"This must be it," he said.

"Yes," I said, "this is it. Wait here while I make an appointment for Monday."

It was a Saturday, so I went in and made an appointment for Monday to do my hair, have a manicure, a pedicure, the whole works.

When I came out, I told the taxi driver, "All right, take me back to the hotel now."

When I calculated we were about a block away from

the Somoza residence, I told him, "Please show me which is the Somoza residence so I'll recognize it the next time I come in a taxi. The house will serve as a reference point to get to the beauty parlor."

"It's not the one I showed you," he told me, "it's this other one."

"Are you sure?"

"Yes, yes," he said. "The police told me: 'It's the gate next door to the timber merchant's warehouse on the corner...'"

And it really was the right house. After three days in Asunción we had located it.

Susana returned to the hotel and disappeared into the ladies' room to take off her makeup. She left the hotel by a side entrance and met Francisco at the cafe they had agreed on. That same day they began a series of passes past the mansion to study the house and to make a plan of the zone. They studied the characteristics of the neighborhood carefully to select certain locations or businesses from which they might keep watch on the house without arousing suspicions. They also took note of the police and security forces stationed in the vicinity.

They had completed their principal assignment without calling attention to themselves, but there were still others to complete.

Francisco went to the real estate agency Susana had called in order to investigate house rentals in Asunción. The house was not for him, he explained, but for some Argentine friends who were planning to move to Asunción in the near future. He was taken to see two or three empty houses in an upper class residential area. Francisco studied each of them closely to see whether or not they had the requisite security features and the degree of privacy necessary to avoid the continuous scrutiny of nosy neighbors. As Susana would be occupying one of the houses later on and he would not, she did not accompany him on the house-hunting expedition but instead used the time to visit a supermarket whose glass front commanded a view of the Somoza residence a block down the street. As luck would have it, the red Falcon escort car pulled out of the Somoza entranceway as she was leaving the supermarket with her shopping bag. It drove past her, and she had time to memorize the license number and to identify Samuel Genie sitting in front beside the chauffeur.

The two of them maintained their honeymoon sightseeing cover and dutifully drove out of Asunción to visit the Jesuit ruins and made the obligatory trip to visit Iguazú Falls. These tours enabled Susana to familiarize herself with the Paraguayan highway system and to verify that there were no permanent police checkpoints in the countryside surrounding Asunción.

One day they drove to the supermarket early, and while Francisco remained in the car in the parking lot, keeping his eyes on the Somoza entranceway, Susana went into the store and bought the makings for a picnic lunch. They drove to Encarnación at the southern tip of Paraguay, just across the Paraná river from the Argentine town of Posadas. They studied the river traffic, the arrival and departure schedules of the passenger boats that plied back and forth between the two towns, and then methodically began exploring all the dirt roads leading off the main highway toward the river. On the fourth try, Francisco parked the car at the edge of the river, folded his arms over the steering wheel and said, "I think this is the place."

There were a few scattered farmhouses to their right, a telecommunications tower across the river in Argentina that would have a red warning light atop it at night, and some fifty meters out in the river before them was a navigation buoy warning of a sunken obstruction in the river.

While Susana assembled the lunch, Francisco busied himself drawing a neat map that showed the identifying landmarks that would enable a small smuggler's launch to find its way to the beach by night. After their leisurely lunch on the beach, Susana completed the map by pinpointing the kilometer marker nearest the turnoff from the main highway.

"Don't worry," she told Francisco, "I could find my way back here blindfolded. I'll bring the others out here when we return."

The honeymoon couple changed hotels twice during the twenty days they remained in Asunción on their scouting mission. Too long a stay in any one hotel would have engraved their faces in the memories of the hotel staff. These changes were primarily for Susana's benefit since Francisco would not be returning to Paraguay. On the final day he drove Susana to the airport and saw her off on her flight to Río. Then he returned the car to the rental agency, caught a taxi to the waterfront passenger terminal and boarded a ferry to take him across the river into Argentina where he had to supervise the delicate business of collecting the arms and concealing them until the time came to smuggle them across the river into Paraguay.

CHAPTER 8

Susana and Francisco had been gone for ten days and the normal training routine continued at the Colombian country house. Ramón's general plan had been drawn up for some time and would only be altered if Susana and Francisco uncovered some unexpected information that made a change necessary. When the pair of scouts completed their initial investigation Susana was to return to Colombia with the answers to Ramón's long list of questions.

Meanwhile Pedro traveled to Argentina to make contact with Mario who had remained in the country during the Videla repression as caretaker of the ERP's hidden arsenal. The two of them had to work out the details of how to transfer the weapons Ramón needed from the place where they were concealed to a new weapons cache as close to the Paraná as possible.

Ramón had decided that the commando group was to be made up of three couples: himself and Julia, Santiago and Susana, and Armando and Ana. Married couples moving to a strange city can rent safe houses without having to answer questions and can make themselves virtually invisible if they choose to do so. The women would not only maintain the necessary cover of domesticity but would also participate in the continual surveillance of the Somoza residence in order to discover a regular pattern in the ex-dictator's movements. In addition, if the operational plan made it necessary, they had the technical training to take an active part in it as efficiently as any man. Finally, they were needed to man the getaway vehicles after the operation was finished.

Ramón, we discovered during our conversations with him, had practical experience in planning and executing delicate

operations requiring steel nerves and split-second timing. He and
three *compañeros* of the ERP, one of whom was Mario Roberto
Santucho, top leader of the movement, had been captured by the
Argentine military in August 1970, and the four were remanded to
the supposedly escape-proof military prison of Trelew, located in
the southern desert of Argentina near the Rawson Navel Base.
Ramón explains:

> At that time they hadn't yet started disappearing people but
> they tortured everyone who fell prisoner. They tortured the
> four of us for ten days.

"What were the tortures like?" we interrupted.

> The usual thing at that time. The *picana eléctrica* (electric
> cattle prod) and methodical beatings. I was black and blue
> from head to foot, but I didn't realize it until they took me
> upstairs for a medical exam. They held me in the pitch-dark
> basement cell and took me out, hooded, only to torture me.
> After the ten days, a judge came to take our statements, and
> then we were held for sixty-three days in solitary confinement.
> They knew exactly who we were, and we were the only four
> of all Argentine political prisoners who were held in solitary.
> During that time, all the political prisoners, many of their
> family members and a number of priests called a hunger strike
> in different churches throughout the country, and at the end
> of sixty-three days, as I said, they took us out of solitary
> confinement.
>
> I was held prisoner for nearly a year. They had
> transferred us to a prison they believed to be escape-proof
> because it was located in the middle of a desert. The town of
> Trelew, which was some twenty-five kilometers distant, had
> an airport with daily flights to Buenos Aires and to southern
> Argentina. On August 15, 1971, a number of us escaped from
> prison in a joint operation mounted by the ERP, the
> Montoneros, and the FAR (Revolutionary Armed Forces.)
> We coordinated the time of our jailbreak with the arrival of
> a plane from the south that was to continue its flight to
> Buenos Aires. A group of four *compañeros* hijacked this plane

in the Trelew Airport and waited for us to arrive from the prison. The operation had to be timed to the split second, and there were all sorts of unknown factors. For example, there were important military bases in the area, such as the naval base at Almirante Rawson. Six of us managed to escape: three from the ERP, one Montonero and two from the FAR. Some of the *compañeros* who were included in the escape plan were trapped inside the airport and taken to the base at Rawson. We commandeered the plane and flew to Chile, where Allende was president. On August 22, the Trelew Massacre took place. It was a national scandal. In response to our escape, the dictatorship assassinated the 16 prisoners who had been recaptured. Eleven of them were members of the ERP, and the rest were from the Montoneros and FAR. This episode also produced a huge popular demonstration against the dictatorship. Seven years later, the coincidence of the taking of the National Palace in Managua with the August 22 anniversary of the Trelew Massacre touched me deeply. To me, it was a sort of retribution.

Anyway, on the day following the massacre, we flew from Chile to Cuba. Two months later, Santucho, Mana, and I, the three ERP members who escaped, returned clandestinely to Argentina via the Chilean border, and I remained inside the country until the beginning of '77.

Ana and Armando were lounging in the shade of the big mango tree at the edge of the garden. Ana, lying at the base of the tree and peering up through the branches, was listening with half an ear to Armando's desultory chatter, but her attention was principally concentrated on one perfect mango gleaming at her, roseate and yellow, far out of reach amid the leaves. There were others, ripe and nearly ripe, dangling in enticing clusters at the same level, but Ana wanted *that* one.

"Let's pick some mangos, Armando," she interrupted his flow of words.

"They're all out of reach," he shrugged. "We've taken all the easy ones."

"That's all right," she sprang to her feet. "Make me a stirrup."

Armando sighed and rose to his feet. Never argue with a woman. He leaned one broad shoulder against the trunk, laced his fingers together and Ana, agile as a teenager, placed one flat-soled sandal in the improvised "stirrup" and, as he boosted her, the other on his outer shoulder. A second later she was balancing on the lowest branch, considering her next move. As she turned to grasp a higher branch, the leather-soled sandal on which she was resting her weight slipped, and she plummeted to the ground off-balance.

"Ay, it hurts!" she moaned, clutching at the damaged ankle. "Ay, Armando, I'm such an idiot."

Ana wept silently in the car on the way to the doctor's clinic in the nearest village, wept inconsolably even after the doctor injected Novocaine in her ankle and gently positioned her foot against the X-ray plate.

"Don't worry, ma'am," he consoled her as he moved to the door of the darkroom with the plate in his hand. "The pain will go away in a few minutes."

"You poor kid," Armando sympathized, passing her his hand-kerchief, "it must hurt like hell."

Ana wiped her eyes, blew her nose and glared at him.

"I'm not crying because of the pain, idiot," she hissed at him, "but because of the project. We were supposed to be the next ones to go in."

Susana was jubilant but did her best to contain it when she met Ramón at the airport.

"Mission accomplished, *compañero*," she announced as they embraced. "We didn't see the man, but I brought the layout of his hideout."

"Tell me." Ramón picked up her bag and they headed out the entrance toward the parking lot. By the time they arrived at the farm, he had mastered every pertinent detail of Susana's trip and was contemplating the next move on the operational chessboard.

Typically, he had not even mentioned Ana's broken ankle, and Susana was shocked to see her friend stretched out on the living room sofa, her leg swathed in a knee-high plaster cast. The other students, under Santiago's supervision, had made the long trek to their wilderness rifle range for a day's target practice, so the three of them could talk openly.

Ramón had brought Ana into the secret before her accident when he saw from her pointed questioning in class that she had decided this was no ordinary operational training course. Because of her documenting skill, Ramón had planned to send her and Armando into Paraguay first in order to prepare for the reception of the rest of the team, but now, with Susana's freshly-garnered information, that might not be as necessary as he had thought.

"Tell Ana about the immigration routine on entering Paraguay," he suggested.

"It's the easiest thing in the world," Susana said. "When you go through passport control they charge you a dollar for a tourist card, which you fill out with your personal data. They keep the original and you keep the copy until you leave the country. They put an entry stamp in your passport and another on your tourist card. That's all there is to it."

"The same stamp on both?" Ana asked.

"Mm, hmm, here it is."

Susana extracted her passport and opened it for Ana. The latter studied the entry and exit stamps attentively for a few minutes.

"If you lose the card, I don't suppose it would be difficult to get another one."

"There's a stack of them at the immigration counter. I snatched two extras to bring back to you."

Ramón waited expectantly for Ana's verdict. He knew she would make any sacrifice, a left leg, say, to not be excluded from the forthcoming mission, but he was also perfectly certain that she would not allow this desire to sway her professional judgment as to the risks they faced in entering Paraguay with falsified documents.

"When you handed in your passport to get your entry stamp, did the immigration officer study the previous visas and stamps to see where you had been earlier?"

Susana shook her head. "He only looked for a blank space to place the stamp."

Ana handed the passport back to Susana but retained the two blank tourist cards.

"A piece of cake," she assured Ramón. "Going in, that is," she corrected herself. "Getting back out will be another matter."

"Fine," Ramón announced, "but we're going to have to alter the plans. Ana was supposed to go in first together with Armando, but she won't be able to travel for at least a month. Julia has just arrived, and we have to give her a refresher course. So you, Susana, are going to have to return almost immediately with Armando to settle in and prepare the reception for the rest of us. Do you see any problems with that?"

Susana frowned thoughtfully. She had just spent three weeks "honeymooning" with Francisco in Asunción, and now she would have to reenter the country with a different "husband." Naturally, they would avoid the hotels where she and Francisco had stayed as well as the Swiss restaurant they had frequented.

"I'll need another passport," she decided, "because I've already entered with this one, and it has the stamps and dates of entry and exit. But I can change my appearance and use dark glasses. There won't be any other problems."

The extra passport was no snag, Ramón knew. Bogotá, one of the major drug and emerald-smuggling centers of the world, was a hive of illegal activities. Everything could be obtained there, so long as the price was right. His revolutionary friends in Colombia would have secure contacts for carrying out the transaction. He exhaled gratefully. The operation was back on track.

Or so he thought at that moment.

When Julia returned from the firing range that evening, the three women delegated the cooking for dinner to the men and retired to their joint bedroom for an informal "ladies' night." Julia had been engaged in another mission for the ERP during the entire training period and had only arrived at the farm a few days before Susana's return from Asunción. This fact did not preoccupy Ramón; Julia already knew everything she needed to know in order to take part in the operation. One of the most experienced militants in the ERP, she had joined the PRT when a high school student of fourteen and had led a clandestine existence in Argentina from the age of nineteen until the security debacle of 1976 forced her to leave the country. Her husband, one of the top leaders of the ERP, had been killed by the military several years earlier.

The following morning, Ana and Susana were awakened by Julia's precipitate dash to the bathroom. They gazed at each other in consternation as they listened to her miserable retching behind the closed door. Some minutes later she reappeared, wan and shaken, to meet their accusing eyes.

"So now you know," she raised her head defiantly. "I'm pregnant, but there won't be any problems. And if you say a single word to Ramón before I decide to tell him, I'll strangle you both."

CHAPTER 9

Susana returned to Paraguay accompanied by Armando during the first week in June, a mere three weeks after she had left the country. The two of them had no problems passing through Immigration and Customs, and they took a room in a comfortable hotel, several cuts above the ones where she and Francisco had stayed. She was "honeymooning" again, this time with Armando, and their cover story was different. Armando's parents were wealthy and had given their son a sum of money to start up in business for himself. He and Susana had decided that there might be more attractive investment opportunities in Asunción than in the competitive, dog-eat-dog environment of Buenos Aires, and Armando wanted to investigate the possibility of starting up a small construction company because he had heard there was a great deal of building activity in Paraguay.

Their first order of business was to rent a house, and Ramón had been specific about what kind of house they needed.

"It has to have four bedrooms and a good location, that is, in a pleasant neighborhood of middle class professionals. You two should settle in and live as if you planned to remain in the country. This should give us freedom of movement and the possibility of getting to know people who may be able to give us more information about Somoza, his friends in Asunción and the places he frequents."

Susana realized that the houses Francisco had looked at were too modest to fulfill the new requirements, so she and Armando rented a car and went to the real estate agency the morning after their arrival to state their requirements. They were willing to pay the rent in dollars, she emphasized.

"I'm sure we'll find exactly the house you are looking for," the office manager was all smiles as he consulted a card index file. "In fact, this might be the very one." He pulled out a card and picked up the telephone. Everything was arranged in a few minutes. The owner himself would meet them at the house within a half hour to show them through it. He gave them the address and located it for them on the city map.

Armando picked up the story:

> I've never had an extra penny in my life, and here I had to act upper middle class and dress as elegantly as possible to go and see this luxurious house. The owner opened the door and looked me up and down when we walked in.
>
> "I've changed my mind and decided not to rent the house," he told me, as if he were saying, "I'm certainly not about to rent it to this mangy hippie."
>
> Later on we saw him on television, and it turned out that he was one of Stroessner's ministers. We were very happy that he had refused to rent it to us.

Susana sighed as they climbed into the car and drove off.

"Look, Gordo, you've got 'proletarian' written all over you. I sometimes wonder how long this cover story of ours is going to hold up."

Armando was crestfallen.

"We might tell people," he suggested, "that my father was a working stiff who saved up, started his own construction company and trained me to take over from the time I was a school kid. Knowing how to build houses is one thing, and knowing how to crook your pinkie when you're drinking tea is another."

Despite their initial setback, the next day they found a house that filled all their requirements. It was the right size, well-located and even boasted a small swimming pool. Best of all, Armando thought, it had an ideal spot for building an arms cache. He signed the six-month rental contract on the spot and handed over the deposit and first month's rent in dollars. The following day he bought a secondhand Peugeot in excellent mechanical shape, and the reception committee for the operation began to function.

"What security benefits did you see in the new house?"

Susana told us:

For three months, we had a house in which four members of the commando team lived, one of whom was our team leader, *compañero* Ramón. We hid the arms there for two months. During the whole time the security of this house was crucial to the success of the operation. We had to manage infinite details to keep the neighbors from suspecting anything, not to mention strangers who might come knocking on the door. We had to keep track of every movement along the block and everything that was happening in the neighborhood and the zone. To play the game in accordance with middle-class rules, I had to hire a part-time maid for domestic service, just like all the other families in the area. I found a married woman who came in two days a week, once for general cleaning and once to do the washing and ironing. She was in the house all day long, from 8:00 in the morning to 5:00 in the afternoon. This called for a special routine during the days she was there, so I was the only one in the house. The only one she knew was myself. Once she caught a fleeting glimpse of my husband (Armando), but she never laid eyes on my relatives (Ramón and Julia).

It made for ridiculous situations. For example, I always had to remind the others not to wash their own clothing, as is our custom in clandestine living. Otherwise, she'd have nothing but bedclothes to wash on Tuesdays. The same thing held true for housecleaning chores. Except for cooking and washing dishes, we had to leave everything else for the maid to clean up. This was hard because we aren't lazy.

I had to use the car regularly, go shopping at the supermarket, answer the telephone in such a way as to maintain our cover story, limit my reading to the sort of trash you always find at news-stands in the Third World, and keep myself well-dressed to receive whoever might come to the door. We maintained friendly relations with the owners, and their son came by once in a while to make sure everything was working or to ask if we needed anything. Once they invited us to dinner because it was their son's birthday. There we met other people from Asunción. Following that party, I had to receive two ladies who came to take tea with me and talk about the marvels of Buenos Aires. For me, that was the most delicate bit. Women are very curious and suspicious and gossipy; I had to watch every word.

Inevitably, we made acquaintances and friends, and this had serious disadvantages because one gets involved in invitations, commitments, telephone conversations, etc. which should be avoided if possible. Outside relationships must be kept on a superficial level.

The house also had a gardener who came every three weeks to do whatever was necessary in the yard. We paid his wages and had to keep a close eye on him, because it was precisely in the back patio that we had constructed the arms cache. He was a pleasant, helpful person about fifty years old, and I tried to make sure he did as little as possible. He would come in the morning, work half a day, eat lunch, pick up his pay, and leave. He never stayed longer. Besides, it was wintertime in Paraguay and the grass grew very little.

"Could you tell us about the arms cache?"

The house had a lovely walled patio in back, with a lawn, swimming pool, flower beds, and a barbecue pit. We had to construct a secure place to hide the weapons, one that could be opened and closed quickly when necessary.

We dug a hole in the corner of the patio where nobody ever stepped. Since Armando was supposedly in the construction business, it was simple to bring some bricks and a sack of cement to the house. We laid a floor and walled the sides of the cavity with bricks and cement so it would stay dry, and we covered it with one of those prefabricated septic tank covers. We placed a flower bed with sprawling plants on top of the whole thing. While we were digging we prayed it wouldn't rain. We couldn't work during the day, so we had to do it at night. We worked hard and finished it in two nights: a total of fourteen or sixteen hours. Armando did a good job. When we stashed the arms in there we wrapped them in plastic for protection against humidity, and while they were there we inspected them twice to make sure there was no deterioration. When we had to move the weapons to the other house, we filled the hole with dirt, got rid of the cover, and left the flower bed sitting there as a gift to the owners of the house.

Meanwhile, Armando also had to live his cover story. His experience in the construction business had been limited to two years as a bricklayer in Buenos Aires before he turned to truck-driving.

"How did you spend your days?" we asked him.

I left the house every day at the same time as if I were going to a fixed job. I always checked the Somoza residence at a different hour each day to see if there was any movement. Susana did the same thing, and sometimes we checked it together. But with only two people, it was impossible to establish an effective surveillance.

Aside from this, I talked to lots of people. I went to look at construction materials, and people supposed I was doing market studies and checking out possible investments in the local construction business. I made friends with people and occasionally invited them home. Both Susana and I have a knack for getting along with people, and nobody ever suspected a thing.

Once we were set up in the house, we had a number of tasks to accomplish before the others arrived. We were able to check out different escape routes and decide on the place where we would receive the arms. The only thing we were unable to accomplish 100 percent was surveillance of the objective. It was very difficult, without any data to work with, to check up on a person who had no regular activity and who could leave his home at any time of day or simply stay put.

What we mostly did was familiarize ourselves with the zone, with the Somoza residence and the routes of access to it. We visited different restaurants to see if they offered conditions that he might find attractive. We couldn't do much more than that. There's nothing in Asunción, absolutely nothing.

"What did you have to do during this period to assure the transfer of arms from Argentina?"

We made three trips to the border and learned that conditions were favorable from an operational standpoint; there were no controls. We passed by a fortress where there was a sentry on duty at the main gate. Automobiles were supposed to reduce speed, but apparently they were never forced to stop. We also made a preestablished contact with Francisco, who crossed over to the Paraguayan side, and there we looked for the spot where the arms would be delivered.

The first site Francisco and Susana had chosen had to be abandoned on the advice of the veteran smuggler with whom Pedro and Francisco had made contact. He told them that spot was dangerous because there was occasional police surveillance from the few houses scattered along the Paraguayan side of the river. Francisco took them to a new disembarkation point that his friend, the smuggler, had assured them was safe.

The spot was easy to locate, because it was one of those zones where smuggling goes on every day. Smugglers have their regular delivery points, and it's not unusual to drive a car to the riverbank to pick up boxes. Contraband is widespread because Paraguay produces nothing, not even food. Everything on the supermarket shelves comes from Argentina or Brazil: butter, ham, spaghetti, everything.

The arms were already packed in three wooden boxes that were marked as automobile repair parts. Armando jotted down the dimensions to make sure they would fit in the trunk of his Peugeot. Since Ramón was expected at the beginning of July, Armando made arrangements with Francisco that the arms would cross the river on July 8. Francisco was to telephone Armando the evening before at 8:00 p.m. to confirm that there was no last-minute change in the plan. On the night of the transfer, when the reception committee could hear the motor of the approaching boat, they were to blink a red light three times to indicate that the coast was clear and to repeat the signal every fifteen seconds until the boat's occupants responded with two white flashes.

Armando also sent word to Osvaldo via Francisco that he should enter Paraguay on July 4th and await a contact in the Linda Vista Bar at 5:00 p.m. Osvaldo was to be the seventh member of the team.

After having set up the essential infrastructure for the operation, Armando and Susana continued their daily reconnaissance of the Somoza residence and they also occupied their time by gathering additional tidbits of information about the former dictator's activities in Paraguay.

Susana told us:

There was a magazine that did a photo story on Somoza in his lakefront house where he went fishing with friends. He had friends in the Stroessner group who were heavily involved in land investment. Somoza bought 20,000 hectares in the Paraguayan Chaco, apparently with the intention of establishing an irrigated cotton plantation there. We also learned that he had acquired huge pieces of land in the state of Goias, in Brazil, quite close to Brasilia. This created problems with the Brazilians, because he bought the land through two dummy partners who acquired them from state officials in Goias. The Somoza property was located in an area that is very rich in minerals.

He also had some minor problems in Paraguay; there were some businessmen who wanted him to make other investments, but Somoza wasn't interested; he wasn't sure he was going to remain in Paraguay. Rumors were circulating that he wanted to move to Punta del Este, Uruguay. He traveled to Buenos Aires regularly to have his heart checked, and he wanted to settle in Punta del Este because that has a high level of *la dolce vita*: a casino, fancy hotels, partying, and women. The possibility that he might pull up stakes and leave for Uruguay was a constant concern of ours during the months we were in Asunción, waiting for the right moment.

CHAPTER 10

"I was walking along in the center of town," Armando recalls, "when I heard someone behind me shouting, 'Gordo! Gordo! Gordo!' It was Julia, who was driving down the street with Ramón when they spotted me."

It is an eloquent commentary on the small size of Asunción's commercial district that Ramón and Julia should stumble across Armando a few hours after their arrival in Paraguay. It was July 2, 1980. They had just checked in at a hotel, rented a car, and decided to take their first look at the target area when they made this fortuitous contact. Their prearranged rendezvous with Armando and Susana was not until the following day in a downtown cafe.

Armando took over the wheel and gave the two newcomers their first tour of the operational zone, pointing out the spots that were feasible checkpoints from which to keep the Somoza residence under observation. He and Susana had succeeded in identifying the four vehicles used by the Somoza entourage and had managed to take down the license numbers of three out of the four. There were two Mercedes Benz limousines, one blue and one white. There was the red Ford Falcon, used by Somoza's bodyguards, and there was a Cherokee Chief for all-purpose use.

After the brief tour, Armando returned to where he had parked the Peugeot and led the others home to surprise Susana. There followed an intensive three hours of debriefing by Ramón as to what new information they had gathered during their three weeks in Asunción and what progress had been made on preparing the arms shipment.

In mid-afternoon, the four of them went out of the house for the ritual shopping expedition to the Korean supermarket a block down the Avenida España from the Somoza residence. Armando had made a list of special items for that night's dinner, which he entrusted to Susana, and the two women entered to do the shopping while Ramón and Armando remained in the car in the parking lot, reviewing possible opportunities offered by the terrain in the target area. Then they got out and chatted on the sidewalk, keeping their eyes on Somoza's entry gate. There was no activity. No one entered or left, either afoot or by auto, during the forty minutes they lounged there.

Armando had a charcoal fire going in the patio's barbecue pit by 6:30 in the evening, and the four of them started passing around the ceremonial gourd of *mate*. When the thermos was empty, Armando broke open an exceptional bottle of Scotch whisky to celebrate the reunion while his genuine River Plate barbecue with all the traditional trimmings, including *chemichurri*, *molleja* and baked potatoes wrapped in aluminum foil, was reaching the point of perfection. Julia put away almost as much of the *asado* as Armando. She was still miserable with morning sickness, she confided to Susana, but she made up for it in the evenings, when she was ravenous.

"Does Ramón know?"

"Not yet, but now that we're here, I'll break the news to him gently."

Ramón and Julia moved into their guest bedrooms that same night and went back the following morning to pick up their bags and check out of the hotel. It was on the way back to the safe house with their bags that Julia confessed to Ramón that she was three months pregnant.

> He looked at me, shocked, but I told him that there would be no problems. Actually, I had very grave doubts. From a human standpoint it was a serious situation. I've known of other compañeras who were pregnant and who had been tortured and thrown in concentration camps. For me, it was important to be able to participate in the operation, because I thought it was extremely valuable for Latin America, for Nicaragua

and for Argentina as well, but I also thought it was unfair of me to risk the life of my unborn child.

Ramón sighed and scolded me for not having told him earlier. He said we would go ahead according to plan and he thought it would work, but he wasn't going to risk anything, and if any complications developed, he intended to ship me out of Paraguay and put me in the hands of a good doctor.

Julia was hopeful that the first three months would be the worst, as was normally the case. What she was mostly worried about was her special responsibility, as Ramón's "wife," for his personal safety. She continued:

I not only felt the weight of my own participation but the fact that I was with Ramón gave me a greater share of responsibility. It's not that some men are indispensable to historic processes, but there are certain individuals whose disappearance would delay the process. Ramón was our sole unifying factor. The possibility of losing him or of something happening to him was a constant weight on all our minds, and we often talked about it among ourselves. He was the most hunted, the best known, the most easily identifiable of us all. I felt that I would have to be ready to do anything in order to save him.

"What cover did the two of you use when you were sharing the house with Armando and Susana?"

We were supposed to be relatives of theirs. We let it be known that Ramón was ill, that he had a serious health problem. We knew that they were in Asunción, so we decided to take a vacation and come visit them. According to the cover story, Ramón fell ill and we had to stay on longer than we had anticipated.

Ramón hardly ever appeared in public. Nevertheless, despite all our security measures, he is a very active person and it was difficult for us to keep him under control. What we tried to do was keep him in the house as much as possible, keep him from participating in checking the Somoza residence too often, and in general, simply trying to keep him out of sight.

"Tell us about Ramón's character."

He is the person who has had the most military experience in the entire history of our party. That, no doubt, gives him an air of self-confidence in any situation. He inspired us with the strong conviction that we were capable of achieving the objective we had set for ourselves. He was never nervous. Sometimes he got mad, but he always gave us the confidence that we were capable of doing the job and that we were going to do it. That was the important thing, a question of honor. We had taken on a commitment, and we had to carry it out. As the weeks went by without our ever laying eyes on the target, we even discussed the possibility of breaking into the house, which obviously would have been suicidal. We would have done it despite the risk of some of us dying, and we would have achieved our aim because we were all convinced that the job had to be done.

Susana expressed herself in the following way about Ramón's personality traits:

For us, he was always the leader of the organization. He was our chief, always, even before we joined up. He is on a different level and has a different way of being. He transmits a great deal of confidence and security, but he also displays lots of human sensitivity. With him, you can talk about any problem, no matter how trivial. When I was feeling downhearted, I'd go to him.

Luckily, nobody in Asunción recognized him. There was a price on his head, an ample reward for anybody who identified him. He disguised himself with dark glasses, a Basque beret, a mustache. Besides, the rest of us did all we could so that Ramón wouldn't have to show his face. He couldn't do the things I did, for example. Not only that, he couldn't walk throughout the center of town, he couldn't frequent certain places. To give him a breath of fresh air, we'd go for a drive out of the city. From time to time, Armando would take him to the outskirts for a steak dinner. But he insisted on participating in the surveillance on the Somoza residence, either by driving past the house at certain hours or by checking from the service station after dark.

After having studied the operational zone in person, it was obvious to Ramón that the team's first priority was to set up a system of surveillance in an attempt to determine some pattern of regularity in Somoza's movements, some element of predictability that would enable them to formulate a concrete plan of operations. Ramón explains the inherent difficulties:

Somoza lived on Avenida España. The stretch where his house was located was called Avenida General Francia, but everybody knew it as Avenida España. It's a thoroughfare that changes its name three times and runs from the upper middle class residential district of Asunción to the center of town. It's a heavily-traveled avenue with traffic controls, because it is one of the two major means of access to the center of the city. The other is four blocks away and runs parallel to Avenida España.

It's in a zone that has practically no commercial establishments, no places that justify any loitering in the area. We could go past the residence on busses or walk past or sit on a bench and chat for periods of up to half an hour. In addition, it was a zone that was heavily controlled by the enemy since it was the area where the majority of Stroessner's ministers and high officials live. Stroessner himself lives close by.

We began to think about operational planning, taking into account the various actions we had foreseen during our preparations: explosives, a bazooka attack, an ambush by sharpshooters. These were different variations according to the possibilities that presented themselves. But the fact was, none of us had yet laid eyes on Somoza.

Since there were now four of us in the country, our first step was to make up a new surveillance plan that would permit us to remain in one spot for a certain length of time, or walking routes that led past the house. There were four places where we could watch the residence: a supermarket, two service stations, and a walking route that kept the house in sight, but none of these could be used safely for more than one hour.

In the service stations we could have the car washed, have it greased, have the oil changed. In the supermarket, while the "wife" did the shopping, her supposed husband could wait outside in the car and watch all possible movements from the parking lot. The walking route consisted of a ten-block stretch which took forty-five minutes, walking slowly. Sooner or later, Somoza would have to go past one of these four places.

We had a map of the zone. First of all, we had to find out whether or not he had some sort of regular movement, so we set up a surveillance plan that consisted of covering all daytime hours for ten days. For instance, we would check the residence on Monday from 8:00 to 9:00, on Tuesday from 9:00 to 10:00, Wednesday from 10:00 to 11:00, Thursday from 11:00 to 12:00, and so forth, using different people each time, of course.

"You were trying to discover a fixed routine?"

Yes. For example, if we spotted him on Tuesday between 8:00 and 9:00 in the morning, then we would check that day and time again, we had to find out whether it was weekly or biweekly. If it didn't happen again, it could be dismissed as accidental.

"And were his movements irregular?"

Yes. We didn't get any results. The only result was that we saw some of his cars coming and going, but at different times and never regularly. We didn't see him.

Armando, who had already been in Asunción for nearly four weeks, sighs when he remembers the surveillance system that the four of them established:

Every other day I took the car to be washed at one gas station or the other. I know it sounds crazy, I told them, but I can't drive a car that has so much as a speck of dust on it. You've never seen a car as well taken care of as that one. It was washed and greased every other day. It wasn't a new car by any means but it looked like new.

There remained the essential preliminary task of bringing the arms from Buenos Aires and delivering them across the river into the hands of those who were waiting for them. Francisco and Osvaldo, who had trained in Colombia together with Pedro, were entrusted with this delicate job. Francisco, who had entered Paraguay in April with Susana to locate the Somoza residence, knew the operational objective. Pedro and Osvaldo, however, had no idea. Ramón had dispatched Osvaldo from Colombia to Argentina before Susana returned from her first trip. Ramón told us:

We sent Pedro and Osvaldo to Argentina to decide how to smuggle a shipment of arms across the river. They didn't know that the target was Somoza. They thought the weapons were for a Paraguayan revolutionary movement. They weren't surprised by this because traditionally we had tried to support the Paraguayan revolutionary movement. In earlier years we had maintained relations with the Uruguayans, Paraguayans and Chileans.

They traveled to Missions province, which borders on Paraguay and Brazil. It is separated from Paraguay by the Paraná River. At certain times of the year the water level drops sharply. When they went to Argentina, they already had a series of meetings scheduled, and we had estimated it would take them a month, more or less, to resolve the problem of how to get the arms across from Argentina to Paraguay.

Pedro and Osvaldo were well-acquainted with the zone and the people who lived there. They made contact with people who earned their living by smuggling merchandise across the river: simple folk who have no other means of survival. The entire zone is poverty-stricken.

They gained the confidence of an old man who rented them his boat and gave them information as to the best places to secretly cross to the other side. As far as he was concerned, they were taking auto repair parts across to sell in Paraguay.

At the same time, Pedro had contact with another compañero who had to bring the arms from Buenos Aires up to the north. This was Mario who had always remained in Argentina. They had their first meeting at a halfway point, which was Paraná, capital of Entre Ríos province in the Argentine littoral. At this meeting they decided how and when the arms would be moved.

Pedro rented a humble shack beside the river to receive them. Since he was from the region, he could do things without drawing attention to himself. Things were arranged so Pedro only had to hold them for twenty-four hours.

"What was the origin of the armament?"

The FAL that Armando was to use in the operation came from the arsenal of the 141st Battalion, as well as the pistols.

The bazooka, the two Ingrams and the M-16 had another origin. At the end of 1975, before the military coup, we bought some special arms in the Paraguayan black market. We had all of these cached in Argentina, but after the military coup in March 1976, the situation changed. We had many problems, but the arms remained hidden because they were never used. Naturally, we had carefully filed off the serial numbers.

Thus it was that when Susana returned to Colombia, we sent Francisco directly to join Pedro and Osvaldo in Argentina, and the three of them made the final arrangements for the transfer of the arms.

"Had Francisco already selected the place where the Arms would be disembarked?

Provisionally, yes, but later it had to be changed in accordance with the advice of the old smuggler and the actual conditions. We discovered Francisco had already talked to the owner of

the boat about the best times to make the trip, and he
arranged the reception site on the Paraguayan side as close
as possible to the hut Pedro had rented across the river. It
was located along a dirt road south of Encarnación.

"How did you know when you were going to receive the
arms?"

This was arranged in a meeting between Francisco, Armando,
and Susana in Encarnación. I arrived after that. Pedro never
entered Paraguay except to deliver the weapons. Before that,
Francisco had two meetings with Armando and Susana in
two different places. One was on a busy corner in the center
of Encarnación and the other in a waterfront bar. As Osvaldo
had already entered Paraguay, Francisco and Pedro were the
two who made the delivery, and after that they took no part
in the operation.

Armando told us about the operation to pick up the arms and
transfer them to the cache that awaited them in the patio of the
house in Asunción:

Ramón and I drove to the disembarkation point, picked up
the arms, and loaded them into the trunk of the car. We had
already established the day and the hour. It was a lonely spot
along a dirt road. There were no problems. The owner of the
boat thought we were bringing in merchandise. Repair parts,
Francisco and Pedro had told him. We didn't talk to the man,
and I don't think he saw us. Nobody stopped us on the return
trip. The sentry at the fortress even saluted us.
     That's another advantage of a corrupt regime: anyone
who smells of money is a gentleman. The police are very
primitive. One day, Ramón and I went to the auto races, and
a policeman flagged us down to ask for a ride. He became
very nervous when he saw we were well-dressed middle-class
types in a good automobile. Money is what is respected in
Paraguay, and a person is treated according to how he dresses.
The same thing happened when we brought in the weapons.
We were gunrunners, but we looked like gentlemen, and we

exploited that fact. Any little problem can be worked out by being firm—the police know that money counts more than anything in that corrupt regime. For ten dollars you can buy a judge. Those things turn one's stomach, but you have to take advantage of them. We returned to Asunción without a single problem.

It was not until the very end of the trip, when they were less than a hundred yards from the safe house, that they encountered the only danger during the entire trip. Armando recalls:

We were nearly there when we spotted a Black Maria parked a block away from the house with ten policemen inside. If we had been returning from the supermarket, we wouldn't have paid any attention, but if they decided to search the car they would certainly have found the arms, which were not concealed.

"Shall we turn in or go on?" Armando asked Ramón. The latter made a lightning calculation as they approached the garage entrance. Was the police van's presence accidental, or were the police waiting to catch them with the goods? If there had been such a flaw in their security, he decided, their goose was cooked either way. Could the old smuggler have betrayed them? Impossible. He was already back on the Argentine bank of the river with Pedro and Francisco and besides, he hadn't the vaguest notion of where they lived in Asunción. No. It was impossible that their security measures had failed.

"We turn in," Ramón said rapidly. "We can't spend the whole night driving around Asunción with those things in the trunk."

The Peugeot turned into the driveway and stopped in front of the garage doors. Ramón got out, unlocked the doors with his key and pushed them wide open. Armando pulled into the garage, and Ramón closed and locked the doors. They entered the house through the inner door without even greeting the two women, ran up to the second floor, and peered out the window of the darkened bedroom that faced the street. Five minutes ticked by while Armando tiptoed down to the living room and explained the possible danger to Susana and Julia. Ten minutes went by, and nobody made a move in the police van. They had picked up the arms at 10:00 p.m., and it was now past midnight. They turned off the living room lights, lit those in the other front bedroom and then those of the upstairs bathroom. Ramón continued his vigil from the darkened bedroom. Ten minutes later all the lights in the house were turned off. The police van pulled away from the curb at 2:00 in the morning, and they never saw it again. By 2:30 in the morning the arms were safely tucked away in the cache, and they remained there, undisturbed, until the next transfer.

CHAPTER 11

The skinny young man with the penetrating gaze sat by himself on the last bench of the passenger launch that plied between Posadas, Argentina, and Encarnación, Paraguay. Osvaldo was dressed in blue jeans and a windbreaker over a short-sleeved shirt. His tennis shoes were well-worn, and the Adidas bag on his lap held all his earthly possessions. His long, thin features remained expressionless as the boat chugged across the Paraná. From time to time, he ran his fingers through his windblown, straight, black hair.

Asunción has to be better than Santa Fe, he told himself, what with Argentine inflation and the shortage of construction jobs. Nevertheless, it was the death of Doña Manuela that had changed his life. Graciela's grandmother left an inheritance to her father, Manuel. It was a small house on the outskirts of Asunción, and the family had decided to move back to Paraguay as soon as Manuel finished his carpentry contract on a new office building in Santa Fe. Osvaldo's bricklaying job had ended in late June, and he had a month, or possibly two, to find a stable job in Asunción before Graciela's family arrived. Then, he sighed resignedly, he would resume his patient negotiations with Manuel which would lead one day to his kneeling beside Graciela before the altar while the priest pronounced the marriage vows.

After disembarking with the other passengers, he went through Customs and Immigration without being noticed, and he caught the 11:00 a.m. bus for Asunción. He ate heartily in a workers' cafe near the bus station and then set off on foot to explore the commercial district and locate the Linda Vista bar, where he had an appointment with Ramón at 5:00 p.m. He felt confident that Ramón would approve the cover story he had been rehearsing as he crossed the river.

Ana felt disconsolate as she swung herself along on crutches from the doctor's office to where the car was parked. For weeks she had been crossing off each day on the calendar taped to the side of the refrigerator at the training school, and just now the old fool of a doctor had blasted her hopes by insisting that her ankle had to remain in the cast for another two weeks. Santiago helped her into the car and placed the crutches between the seat and the door.

"I can't take it any longer, Flaco," she exploded while he started the motor. "We're the last ones at the ranch, and there's nothing to do there. Why don't we consult another doctor in Bogotá, and I'll tell him I broke the ankle a week earlier?"

Santiago agreed with her. He was as impatient to get going as she was. They packed as soon as they returned to the ranch, cut off the electricity, closed up the house and headed for Bogotá that same afternoon.

They chose a young bone specialist, one of the new generation. He listened sympathetically while Ana explained the urgency of traveling to Uruguay where Santiago had a job awaiting him. He accepted the date of the accident and agreed that if she were very careful it might be possible to remove the plaster cast a week early. He took an X-ray of the ankle, and after an anguished five-minute wait he emerged from the darkroom and announced that the bone had knit solidly and the cast could be removed. As he cut away the plaster he instructed her in the rehabilitation exercises she should do each day.

It was awful, Ana recalls. My leg was all hairy and dirt-encrusted. I bathed it and shaved with Santiago's razor. I went to a rehabilitation center for one day, and afterwards Santiago gave me the exercises. I traveled with him to Paraguay a few days after the cast was removed.

When Ana and Santiago arrived in Asunción on July 16, Osvaldo had been job-hunting along Avenida España for nearly two weeks. Neither of the gas stations needed an assistant, and there were no openings at the Korean supermarket. The manager of the bowling alley offered to hire him as a pin-boy, but that was an inside job which would not have allowed him to keep watch on the Somoza residence. Osvaldo moved from his modest hotel to a cheap boarding-house, and except for his periodic contacts with Ramón, he stayed away from other members of the team. During the day, he was able to spend more time than the others loitering in the area on the lookout for any activity at the Somoza mansion, but unfortunately there was nothing to report.

Ana went on with her story:

We came in as Uruguayans. There are lots of Uruguayans in Paraguay. We were there for economic motives and were planning to stay some months to try to start a business. Santiago was very good at inventing cover stories and improvising a line of chatter to accompany them. Besides his physical presence—he was tall and elegant—he got along with people very well. It was mid-July when we arrived, and Asunción was filled with tourists. There were no hotel rooms available. At the tourist bureau there were private parties who waited there to offer tourists the rental of a bedroom in their own home. We accepted one such offer and stayed in a private home for one week while we arranged to rent a house. We developed a good relationship with the man and his wife since we ate breakfast with them every day. Santiago told them about our plans to set up a business, and the man advised us not to hand over all our investments at once, because Paraguay was full of crooks. We rented a blue Volkswagen, which we kept the whole time we were there, renewing the contract every two weeks.

Armando recalls:

When Santiago arrived with Ana we set up an appointment in the center of town, and the first thing he asked me was: "When are we going to do it?"

"How are we going to do it, you mean," I told him, "since we haven't even seen the man yet."

Five weeks had gone by since we established the surveillance routine, and nobody had laid eyes on Somoza. There were times that we even doubted he lived there.

Santiago was bitter about our failure, and that very evening we reorganized the surveillance between the six of us.

Ana continued her story:

When we finally rented the house, we ran into one of those nasty surprises that are typical in this kind of situation. We had been investigating different neighborhoods, and when we saw the place we finally rented, it had a sign with the name and number of the rental agency. We went there and told the woman manager that we were interested in looking at that particular house. She started gabbling about terrorism. She told us about the guerrilla girl who had placed a bomb under Cardoza's bed in Argentina. The woman had lived for a long time in Argentina; she was an ambassador's wife. She told Santiago, "How very strange. Your accent sounds Argentine."

My own accent is less noticeable, because I'm from Buenos Aires, but Santiago comes from the interior and has a pronounced accent.

He told her that there was a zone in Uruguay where everybody spoke that way. The manager made us wait until nearly closing time, because the owner of the house was coming to show it to us. It was almost 6:00 when she opened the door and said, "Here are some compatriots of yours who want to look at your house."

While we'd been with the Paraguayan woman, Santiago was the one who led the conversation, but now he grabbed my arm and muttered, "I'm not going to open my mouth. You do the talking."

The woman was discreet. The only thing she asked was if the two of us would be alone in the house. We didn't talk during the drive, except when she asked Santiago about his work in Uruguay.

"What company do you work for?" she asked him.

Santiago answered something that sounded like "RUY—

Y—Y," a slurred word that nobody could understand. That was all he said during the twenty minutes it took us to get there. Once we were inside the house, she asked us how we liked it. Santiago gave me a look as if to say, "You tell her."

The following day we went to sign the contract with the manager of the rental agency, and we never saw the owner again.

Santiago and Ana moved into their new house, and Osvaldo kept looking for work along Avenida España, but he found nothing that would permit him to keep the Somoza mansion under observation. All the team members concentrated now, not on establishing a routine pattern of the comings and goings of the former dictator, but simply on trying to catch the first glimpse of him to verify that he did indeed live in his Asunción fortress. Despite the inclusion of Santiago and Ana in the surveillance team, another week of increasing frustration dragged by while Somoza remained invisible.

"Didn't you start feeling desperate when Somoza didn't appear a single time during nearly six weeks of checking?" we asked Ramón.

He replied:

After we'd gone forty days without seeing Somoza, naturally we were deeply concerned. We changed the manner in which we conducted the surveillance as much as possible, and week by week we analyzed different possible variations for locating him. We almost hypnotized ourselves into believing that things would change during the coming week, but as day after day went by without results, we realized that things were going to be more complicated than we had thought when we started the checks. We began to worry about the length of our stay in Asunción and about our repeatedly frequenting places where we couldn't fully justify our presence.

I received daily reports from the compañeros, and I asked them to make sure they weren't attracting unwanted attention. Our lack of success began to affect us psychologically. Some of the compañeros began to feel that they were under suspicion and being watched. We analyzed each such case in minute detail, and if we didn't arrive at a clear conclusion that the incident was accidental, we suspended their activity until we knew what was happening.

It was in the midst of this nerve-wracking tension that Armando left his house at 8:00 a.m. the morning of July 22. He was going to have the Peugeot washed in the second gas station, and this would permit him to observe the residence for at least 45 minutes.

I was driving along the street that passes behind the Somoza mansion when I saw a white Mercedes with a red Ford Falcon following it. It was completely accidental. I saw the two cars when they were about 100 meters away from me, and I thought it might be them. I stared at the white Mercedes as it came toward me, and there was our target in the front seat beside the driver, looking every inch a dictator. I only knew him from photos, but to see him sitting there fat, white, and puffy, was like being struck by lightning, and I exclaimed, "It's him."

I had to return to the house because I was trembling like a leaf, and I told Ramón. I couldn't explain things very clearly because I was so overcome. Ramón was exhilarated. After all, forty days had gone by and this was the first time any of us had seen him.

We began grasping for conclusions. In our regular checks we had never discovered that the house had another exit through a gate that led into an alleyway at the rear of the house. From the way he was dressed—-he was wearing a sweatshirt—we deduced that he was on his way to do some sort of exercise. Another of our conjectures was that he used this rear gate for security reasons, since the other cars went out the front gate to do the shopping, the visiting, or whatever. On the basis of these deductions we changed some of the surveillance patterns to try to cover the back street.

The team's morale was high once again. Ramón held a clandestine meeting with Osvaldo and gave him instructions to also look for a job along the street running behind the Somoza residence. There is a grain of truth in the saying, "It never rains but it pours." The following morning, Susana and Julia were walking past the mansion at 8:00 in the morning on the way to the supermarket when they spotted Somoza.

Susana remembers the episode this way:

> The house had a white wall at the front yard with two immense black gates set into either end. We walked past the first gate and as we were walking alongside the wall to reach the other gate, it opened and out glided the limousine. We had to stop while the car was crossing in front of us, and there he was. It was awful because he was virtually within arm's reach. He looked at us, and we stood there, petrified.
>
> Afterwards, we passed along those sidewalks so often that people got to know me. I went by much more frequently than Julia. Julia attracts a lot of attention, because of her eyes, because of her height. She is much more easy to identify than I am. I'm an ordinary-looking sort. I passed by as if I might be one of the neighbors. The staff that worked at the Somoza mansion—the bodyguards, the service personnel—started flirting with me. They had come to recognize me. Sometimes I'd pass by on the other side of the street, allowing me to see from a greater distance in case they opened the gate, and they'd still whistle at me. Armando told me, "Go ahead and smile back at them. We still don't know whether we might have to go in after him."
>
> It might turn out that we'd have to go to the house to offer some sort of service or to ask a question. Julia had thought of the possibility of dressing up and asking for an interview with the man. Ana also passed by the house frequently, but she was in Asunción a shorter time than the rest of us. She entered last and was the first one to leave in order to come back in at the end.
>
> We accidentally saw Somoza again that very evening, but the irregularity of his comings and goings were nerve-wracking. Our surveillance had to be extremely casual. On

Saturdays and Sundays there were no businesses open to justify our presence. As time went by the possibilities were fewer. If to this you add the fact that you can't let your face be seen four times a day, you can see that the surveillance had to be very spotty. For that reason, we had to keep changing the plan as we went along.

Two days after Susana and Julia spotted Somoza, Osvaldo had a stroke of luck, and he got in touch with Ramón to tell him the good news:

> I went around looking for work as close as possible to the mansion, and behind the Somoza house there was another house under construction that was nearly finished. I thought there might be a job opening for a bricklayer or a painter. Since the house was almost finished, I decided to be a painter. At the moment I applied, the contractors were away, and I had to wait until the end of the month for one of them to return. The possibility was open, because they were going to have to hire painters and painters' assistants.
>
> The place had a good view of the rear entrance to the residence, but the front of the house was not visible. I had to wait until the contractors returned so I took advantage of that period to go by the job and spend a half hour or an hour every day talking to the workers drinking *mate*, wandering about, and keeping my eye on the big house.

Things didn't work out as the team had foreseen. The rear entrance to the Somoza residence turned out to be a false lead. Except for the first time that Armando saw the dictator, he was never again seen entering or leaving by that exit. If Osvaldo had accepted a job as a house painter, he would have lost his usefulness to the team.

CHAPTER 12

"The central problem is that Somoza doesn't have a fixed schedule for his comings and goings. All his movements seem capricious."

Ramón spoke to the other three as if he were thinking aloud. He was looking at their chart of surveillance results: a sheet of graph paper with four or five red "X" marks distributed at random over the page.

"Aside from his irregularity," he continued, "there is the inadequacy of our surveillance timetables. He could leave and enter the residence several times a day without any of us being on hand to record it. Even if Osvaldo's job works out, he will only be able to cover the rear entrance, and we'd have the same problem as ever with the main entrance. Obviously, what we need is a fixed observation post from which we can watch the entrance continuously throughout the day. Does anyone have any ideas?"

There was an uncomfortable silence, which Julia broke with a tentative suggestion:

"There is a stoplight at the corner where the supermarket is located, and there are always half a dozen street-vendors selling fruits and tomatoes to people in the stopped cars. None of us has the right appearance to pull it off, but maybe Osvaldo might..."

Armando considered the idea and then shook his head firmly.

"Those people are very poor, and they'll defend that spot where they eke out a living against any intruder. Undoubtedly, they would look on Osvaldo as their mortal enemy. But there are also three news stands in the area. One of those would be ideal if Osvaldo could land a job there."

It was Ramón's turn to say no.

"He's already tried his luck," he said, "and there are no openings."

"What if Osvaldo offers to buy one of the stands?" Armando insisted. "I've noticed that one of them is poorly managed. It's closed a good bit of the time."

"Is that so?" Ramón became interested. "Something like that could offer possibilities."

That same night, Ramón met with Osvaldo, and the two of them had a long discussion about the best way to approach the owners of the three kiosks.

Osvaldo picks up the thread of the story:

> I made friends with the news-stand owners. Two of the stands were about 150 meters from the Somoza residence in opposite directions, and the third about 250 meters away.
>
> The closest ones would have been ideal from our standpoint, but they were also doing better economically. They had more magazines, more cigarettes, more of everything.
>
> Since the one 250 meters away also had a view of the mansion and wasn't doing well economically, I went to talk to the owner, and he said yes, there was a possibility something might be worked out. He wasn't the sole owner but had a partnership with another man, and the two of them had another news-stand in the very center of Asunción. At first I offered to buy the stand, but he said no, he didn't want to sell. Then I proposed that I would invest money in it. I offered to buy more magazines, cigarettes, and things like that. I told him I would fix the sidewalk, which was broken, and I'd install electricity so we could stay open nights.
>
> He was tempted by the offer and said he would give me a two-month period, during which I could keep all the profits and recoup some of my investment. After the two months were up we would sign a contract under which I would keep ten percent of the profits. He even started thinking about putting up another stand in a spot that he felt was a better location. I accepted everything in principle but insisted that I had to work there at least two months in order to recover

part of the money I was investing. He agreed, and we didn't even sign a contract.

I started working there and saw the location was very good. I kept the kid who had been running the stand as my assistant so as not to leave him in the street, which would have been a dirty trick. I went to visit his home, made friends with the family, and sometimes even spent the night there. But I stayed on at the boarding house. I made lots of friends: girls who worked as servants, people who lived in the area and who bought papers and magazines regularly and even asked me to extend them credit. I even befriended policemen who were guarding a Paraguayan government official who lived a few doors away. And all the time I was watching for Somoza's movements.

I'm sure the owner had the intention of taking the kiosk away from me afterward, but I accepted the contract. A part of it was in writing, but the rest was simply my verbal guarantee that I would take care of the stand, fix the sidewalk and install electricity. Afterwards, we were supposed to go halves in a new kiosk. He was going to put up half the money for that, and we'd split the profits. But, of course, that never happened.

While Osvaldo was involved in preliminary negotiations with the owner of the kiosk, the rest of the team continued with the daily surveillance and spent much of their free time reviewing possible plans for carrying out the operation once they were able to fix the target at a certain time and place.

The high-class restaurants of Asunción seemed worth investigating, since the team already knew that Somoza dined out from time to time at the most exclusive ones. One day, for example, while Ramón, Julia, and Santiago were having lunch at a modest restaurant in the center of town, they saw the white Mercedes Benz, the red Ford Falcon, and Samuel Genie, Somoza's chief of security, outside a much more elegant restaurant on the opposite side of the street. Genie remained there while Somoza and his friends finished their lunch. The three waited two hours for the dictator to appear, but they never saw him.

The following day, Ramón sent Santiago and Julia to lunch at that other restaurant to take note of the interior floor plan and the location of the other exits. Ramón could not enter that establishment since the owners were an Argentine couple who might possibly recognize him.

Julia said:

I remember that Santiago had bought a gray suit. He was tall and very elegant. Like Susana, he's a person who knows how to behave in any company. If he's in popular surroundings, he's at ease and talks like everyone else, and if he's in a high-class spot like that restaurant, he blends in with the background.

I told him, "You're super-elegant."

He was wearing the suit he'd be wearing to the airport for the getaway.

"You don't look like a revolutionary," I teased him, "you look like a gentleman."

While we were looking the place over and eating, he asked me how I felt, how I was getting along. Santiago was a very sensitive person, and a pregnant woman can be highly impressionable. At that point I wasn't even sure I wanted another child. I had gone through that before, living clandestinely with my first child, and I asked him, "What if I have to return to Argentina with another baby? I don't want to run that risk."

He told me that a revolutionary had to experience mother-hood. What worried me was that, as my pregnancy advanced, however hard I tried, I might become a burden to the other *compañeros*. I talked all these things over with him. We'd known each other for a long time. Years before when he'd received a leg wound in a guerrilla confrontation, the *compas* brought him to my house to recuperate. Santiago was a very warm human being, and this conversation did me a lot of good.

There was another high-class restaurant in Asunción that Somoza also frequented, and one evening Ramón proposed that the two couples have dinner there to check out the floor plan. As usual on such occasions, Susana supervised Armando's attire.

"We have to dress elegantly, *che*," she advised him. "Put on your blue suit with a striped shirt and gray tie."

She went upstairs to dress and found Julia with a worried frown on her face pondering her scanty wardrobe. She held up a fashionable dinner frock and wailed, "This is the only decent thing I have, and it doesn't fit me any more."

At Susana's insistence, she tried it on again, and it was true: the passing weeks had made a difference, and Julia was now graced with a perceptible protuberance in front.

Susana sighed and started searching through the remaining dresses.

"Wear this," she decided, handing Julia a pair of lounging pajamas.

"I can't, Susana. I bought that to be comfortable around the house."

"These are very *in*, *che*," Susana assured her. "With a gaudy necklace and your hoop earrings you'll be perfect."

"Ramón doesn't understand women's fashions. He's going to be mad."

"Then leave your coat on."

As they descended the staircase, Susana gave Armando a critical once-over.

"Where's your vest?" she asked.

Armando fidgeted.

"With all this inactivity," he confessed, "I seem to have gained a few pounds, and I can't get into it."

"Go and put it on," Susana ordered him. "We've got to show some class."

"But, Susana," Armando protested, "it's too tight and terribly uncomfortable."

"Go and get into it, proletarian," Susana said in a steely voice, and that was that.

He was noticeably uncomfortable when they took their seats at the restaurant table, but when he started studying the menu his face lit up, and he ordered an entree of spaghetti with cheese, followed by a serving of the River Plate's justifiably famous "baby beef": a thick, juicy sirloin that fills the entire serving platter.

He fell to with gusto when the first course arrived and started shoveling down the spaghetti.

"Armando," Susana hissed, "don't eat so fast. It's not elegant."

He slowed down to a moderate pace, and as the small mountain of spaghetti steadily disappeared, Ramón counseled him, "Careful, Gordo. Don't eat too much or you'll split your vest."

Armando looked up from his plate indignantly.

"Why should I deprive myself of this delicious meal?"

"Armando," Susana seconded Ramón, "don't eat any more. A person of refinement never finishes everything that's on his plate."

Armando looked around at the plates of the other diners.

"That's horrible," he said.

Julia, seated across the table from him, was by now struggling to hold back a giggling fit.

"Please, Armando," she chimed in, "if you pop a button, you'll take out one of my eyes."

Unfortunately, this comment drew Ramón's attention to her.

"Why don't you take off your coat, *che*?" he suggested. "Nobody else in here is wearing one."

"No," Julia turned serious, "it's chilly in here."

"It's not elegant," Ramón insisted. "Take it off."

"The thing is," she said, "I'm wearing an outfit that's in very high fashion, only it looks like pajamas."

"That's okay," Ramón said, "just take off your coat."

Julia stood up and slipped out of her coat. Ramón's jaw dropped as he stared at her, horrified. Armando, red-faced but relieved that he was no longer the center of attention, puffed out his cheeks and exhaled heavily.

"She really did it; she came in her pajamas," Ramón muttered disbelievingly. "She's out of her mind."

Julia sat down again.

"It isn't pajamas. What makes you think I'd come in a pair of pajamas?"

"Don't get up and go to the ladies' room," Ramón warned her. "And put your coat back on."

"No, Ramón," she answered reasonably, "I'm not going to put it back on. I don't want to draw attention to myself."

Ramón told us:
Osvaldo started working at the news-stand around the 12th of August, Since he's a very extroverted type, he was surrounded by Paraguayans from the beginning. He sold pornographic magazines to the policemen, and he'd let others stand there and read magazines without paying for them. The kiosk was located about 250 meters away from the Somoza mansion. It was a place Somoza had to pass when he headed for the center of town. There were only two possibilities: either he had to continue down Avenida España, or he had to turn off at the corner where the news-stand was located.

After the 22nd of July, we saw Somoza four times in a single week, and we were elated. But after that, we didn't see him again until August 12—the day that Osvaldo started working at the stand. Osvaldo was there from 6:00 a.m. until 8:00 p.m. and the very first day he saw Somoza at 12:00 noon and again at 4:00 p.m. Once again we became highly enthused. We drew up a movement chart for all the daylight hours. From then on, Osvaldo saw him practically every day until August 21.

Susana added:
Osvaldo's history links him directly to northern Argentina. He knows the Paraguayan character and even speaks some Guaraní. He has dealt with them all his life. He's very street-wise; he's a hustler, a wheeler-dealer who spends his entire life buying and selling things. You can tell by looking at him that nobody's going to take him for a ride. All his personal characteristics made him the ideal person to take over that strategic observation post.

Once he took over the news stand, he did all the checking, and we were no longer needed. One or another of us would go by there every day. For instance, I would pass by in the car, stop, and Osvaldo would sell me a magazine. Inside there would be a message for Ramón, a report on what he had seen during the day. To all outward appearances, we didn't know each other.

Ramón picked up the story:

We started refining certain details. For example, Osvaldo has a terribly penetrating gaze. You can feel the nape of your neck bristling when he looks at you. To correct this, we started playing a game once he took over the kiosk. We would pass by in an automobile, and afterwards he would have to tell us how many were in the car and where each of us was sitting, plus any other unusual details, and he would have to do all this in such a way that we couldn't tell he was watching us. He had to learn how to observe everything without being obvious about it, and he learned how to do it successfully.

Osvaldo's news-stand resolved the most crucial problem: that of spotting Somoza any time he left his house and observing what route he took. The team was jubilant, and Ramón began planning the next operational step. But on Thursday, August 21, Osvaldo did not spot him, nor on the next day, nor during the weekend. As the days went by, little by little the apprehension grew until it became almost an overwhelming conviction: Somoza had left Asunción.

CHAPTER 13

Even before Osvaldo resolved the problem of keeping Somoza's movements under surveillance from the newspaper stand, Ramón and the others had considered and discarded various plans for carrying out the operation. One of these involved buying a truck, filling it with vegetables, hiding the arms among the boxes, and going from door to door selling fresh vegetables along Avenida España until the objective passed by. A variation on this was to have a covered truck parked on the avenue with the armed commando team inside, awaiting an opportunity to strike. A third possibility was to wait for Somoza on a street corner with the submachine guns and pistols hidden in shopping bags. This last idea was immediately rejected because they didn't know whether or not Somoza's limousines were bullet-proof. The first two ideas were also rejected because in this area, teeming with security guards, a truck would sooner or later attract attention, and the arms would speak for themselves.

"We thought of a whole series of possibilities," Armando recalled, "and if he'd had any regularity of movement, any one of them would have worked.

The nucleus of the problem was the need to wait in a secure place without attracting anyone's attention until the target appeared.

As a last resort, the team seriously discussed the possibility of bursting into the Somoza residence at a moment when they were certain the former dictator would be found there. Santiago thought of making a surreptitious entry into the lumber yard next door to study it as the point from which to launch the assault. Late one night he walked down Avenida España to try to break into the place, but when he was within half a block of his objective, he was stopped by a patrol car and asked to show his documents. Needless to say, this incident dampened the enthusiasm of all of them with regard to a suicide attack.

The fact was that Somoza had disappeared, and the possibility that he had decided to leave Asunción for Punta del Este, Uruguay, seemed most plausible. The continuing tension of not knowing his plans mounted each day, along with the other problem of increasing boredom. Asunción offered so few diversions that one night, Julia, Ramón, Armando and Susana ran into Osvaldo coming out of one of the principal movie theaters as they were entering for the last showing. They settled into their seats during the intermission, and just as the lights went down, Santiago and Ana walked in and took seats a few rows ahead of them. The picture, Osvaldo remembers, was *A Distant Bridge*.

On another of the rare occasions in which the whole team got together in Armando and Susana's house to review operational plans, it occurred to Osvaldo to announce on the spur of the moment that it was his birthday. That was sufficient to transform the meeting into a party. The inspiration probably came to him, Osvaldo confessed to us, because he had to hide in the back seat of the Peugeot on the way to the meeting, and this made him feel that he was the loneliest of the whole group.

Osvaldo continued:

We were going to have a barbecue and talk things over to evaluate the entire operation. At that moment the inspiration hit, and I thought of a way to forge a stronger link with all of them. I had to be working at the kiosk most of the time. It wasn't work, really, because I could sit down. It wasn't a sacrifice. The fundamental problem, which I didn't realize at the time, was the tension that kept building up. I wanted to be together with them to talk about the operation and get the whole thing off my chest. I had a lot of other friends and acquaintances, but with them I couldn't say a word about what was on my mind.

When the others began to heap improvised birthday gifts on him—Armando gave him a radio-cassette player he had once admired—Osvaldo's revolutionary rectitude imposed itself, and he confessed that it wasn't really his birthday; he had simply wanted to pep things up a bit. Despite his confession, all the others insisted that he keep the gifts.

Even though Somoza hadn't reappeared, during the meeting Ramón insisted on continuing to develop plans for the final operation. It was obvious, he said, that there was no way to improvise a place in which to carry out the operation. But, just as the surveillance problem had been solved by installing Osvaldo in a fixed observation post, so they had to find a fixed spot where the team could await their opportunity to carry out the plan.

One of the few predictable movements they had been able to establish with respect to Somoza was that every time he left his house in the Mercedes Benz, he would continue straight down Avenida España instead of turning off to the right or left at the intersection where the stop-lights were located. Along the whole stretch that led to the center of town there were only two houses for rent. One of these, as they could see through the curtainless windows, was unfurnished and presented a series of problems of expense and security if they were to rent it as an operational post. The other seemed to be at least partially furnished, but it was much larger than the first: ideal for an embassy residence or the home of a rich industrialist. The key problem was how to approach the owner of the house. What they needed was a convincing cover story to justify renting so large a house for so short a time.

"Does anyone have any ideas?"

Ramón leaned back in his chair and waited. After a pause, during which the others were figuratively scratching their heads, Julia spoke up. "I have a crazy idea, but it's just outlandish enough that it may work. It so happens that in one of his most recent albums Julio Iglesias has three songs about Paraguay that have become fairly popular..."

She outlined her plan to the others and received an enthusiastic response. They examined it from various angles and thought of possible complications before approving it unanimously.

The elegant brunette with a ponytail and large cat eyes registered at the next-best hotel after the Guaraní an hour after the morning plane from Buenos Aires landed at Asunción. She installed herself in her room, made a telephone call, and arranged a date for that same afternoon. But let's have Julia tell the story in her own words:

> My tummy was bulging a little, so I bought an outfit that was loose-fitting but very stylish.
>
> I made a telephone call from the hotel, and the owner agreed to meet me at the house. It was an ostentatious home, very luxurious, with four bathrooms, many rooms, and a large swimming pool.
>
> It needed a lot of furniture, and no ordinary tourist could think of renting it. Who might be capable of doing so? A diplomat, a rich businessman, or a pop artist. Since Julio Iglesias had recorded three Paraguayan songs, we invented the idea that he was going to make a film in Paraguay and he required a comfortable home while the shooting was underway.
>
> The woman was with her husband. She was Chilean, and the husband was there to place his signature on the contract, nothing more. She was there to handle the arrangements, do all the talking, dicker for the best deal, everything. She was one of those bourgeois females who are very sure of themselves. Snooty. She began by asking me who I was. I told her I was Argentine and that we wanted to rent the house for a special purpose. I didn't want to start off by telling her it was for Julio Iglesias. I started by asking the price, whether they themselves had lived in the house. The woman was very composed, and the questions she asked me were tactful, but finally she asked me, "But why do you want *this* house?"
>
> Then I told her, "I'm going to tell you the truth, Madame, but I beg you to observe the greatest discretion, because for us it is a very delicate situation, and if it's mishandled it might even affect your house."

I gave her this big buildup, and she was saying, "Yes, yes, of course, certainly, but who is it for?"

"Very well," I said, "it's for Julio Iglesias who is going to film a picture here in Paraguay."

"Uy!" she said, "I can't *be-l-ieve* it! My house is going to be famous."

"I thought to myself: "It most certainly is, but not for the reason you think." It was terribly funny, and I had trouble keeping a straight face. When I said "Julio Iglesias" her face changed, everything changed.

"Uy!" she said. "My daughter lives in Chile. Perhaps she can come to meet Julio Iglesias. Will we have a chance to get to know him?"

"Of course," I told her. "However, we'll need at least a month to get the house ready before his arrival. You know how all these performers are. But please, we need the strictest discretion. Otherwise, we'll have crowds of people all the time, and your garden will be trampled in the crush. It's all right to let it be known that Julio Iglesias is in Asunción, but not to let anyone know where he is staying. If you want to drop by and have a chat with him, we have no objections whatsoever."

The woman was enchanted. She invited me to her home to arrange the contract. Ana had prepared documentation for me: a letter in which Julio Iglesias' representative authorized me to rent a house for him, and another plasticized card accrediting me as a member of the Association of Argentine Artists. Much later we learned that this association had ceased to exist when Ramón was still a boy, but she knew nothing about that and accepted everything as gospel truth. She was completely fascinated. She asked for my local address to be able to reach me, and I knew she wanted to confirm what I had told her and that she intended to call me. That is why I registered at one of the best hotels and stayed there for two or three days. She did telephone me, we signed the contract, and I told her I had to return to Argentina.

The elegant young lady with the single, stylish, traveling bag checked out of the hotel two hours before the noon plane left for Buenos Aires. The bellboy who carried her bag out to the curb received a lavish tip, and she rewarded the doorman, who asked if he could hail her a cab, with a dazzling smile.

"No thanks," she replied, "some friends are picking me up. In fact, here they are now. What perfect timing."

Armando deposited her bag in the trunk of the Peugeot while she climbed into the rear seat beside Ramón, who was wearing his Basque beret and dark glasses. Julia opened her handbag as Armando pulled away from the curb, and she handed the contract to Ramón with a flourish.

"It's ours," she grinned triumphantly. "Operational Base Alpha."

The last hurdle had been overcome, and with a fixed base along Somoza's normal path of travel, the team was now prepared to finalize plans for springing their lethal trap on the ex-dictator when—and if—he should reappear.

Their newly-rented mansion, while ideally located for their mission, was located, figuratively speaking, in the lion's mouth. Ramón explains:

> The neighbor on one side was the Paraguayan Minister of Tourism, and the two neighbors on the other side were personal friends of Stroessner. Stroessner's own mansion was only 200 meters away. It was a very selective zone: we were 400 meters from the Army General Staff building and 300 meters from the American Embassy. There was a permanent security guard in front of Stroessner's residence. We each had to be extremely careful about our movements so as not to arouse the slightest suspicion.

"How much did the rental cost you?" we asked.

> A total of $4,500. The price was $1,500 per month, and we had to pay three months in advance. We had to hire a watchman so we ourselves would not be too much in evidence. Julia had told the owner that sometime soon electricians would come in to arrange the interior lighting in accordance with Julio Iglesias' requirements. But we were already reaching the end of August, and Osvaldo hadn't seen hide nor hair of Somoza since the 20th.

CHAPTER 14

Armando and Susana had been living in the Asunción house for three months, and Armando's cover story was wearing dangerously thin. Because of his supposed investment activities, he had not been able to avoid making an increasingly wide circle of acquaintances. As the weeks went by, it was inevitable that sooner or later these occasional friends would begin to ask themselves, "When in the world is old Armando going to start up his construction business?"

Susana describes the building tension during this phase:

Something that kept us on pins and needles was the delay. The operation had been planned to take two months at most. The imponderables are always out of one's hands, though. The time arrived when the delay became intolerable. We thought we'd have to replan everything so we could stay longer. Our cover story had been designed to hold up for two months, and it did so perfectly. The proof is that it held up for three.

All the plans we had laid, our cover stories, all our movements—the entire situation was wearing thin. There was the ever-present danger of making a mistake that would create security risks. The fundamental security problem didn't simply concern our own physical integrity but the possibility that we might blow the operation for good. We were eaten up by anxiety. We could fall into voluntarism, for example, and tell ourselves, "No, since nothing has gone wrong, stop worrying and let's keep on." One example was the house. We might be able to hang on for five months, but probably not. It took days of increasing tension to work out the problem.

We had meetings, and we talked and we thought. We finally brought a proposal to Ramón, who was the one to make the final decision.

We decided that Armando and I had to leave the house and disappear from Asunción for a while to "cool off." We had a justifiable reason: that the investment possibility wasn't working out, and we were going to see if we could start a business somewhere else. Besides, I said, I just don't like this country. This was another valid argument. At a certain, middle-class level, among the couples we knew, things functioned that way. The wives visit Buenos Aires, and they don't want to keep on living in Asunción. We were going to Brazil because it is a beautiful country with lovely cities. There we could invest in a business and lead the sort of lives we wanted to. All this was perfectly credible because it was real. The couples we knew thought that way, and they were even envious of us.

We said good-bye and we took off, but the problem that persisted and caused continual tension was that all the rest of the time we were in Asunción we had to avoid any contact with the people we had gotten to know.

Leaving the house wasn't simply a matter of cutting off the electricity and returning the key to the landlord. Ramón and Julia had to find other quarters and, above all, a new cache for the weapons, and the transfer had to be carried out without running any risks. The house that Santiago and Ana had rented was the logical solution for the new hiding place. Santiago solved the problem by removing the back of the living room sofa, depositing the arms inside and then replacing the upholstered back.

Ramón and Julia moved to a small temporary apartment. Armando sold the Peugeot to a car dealer, and Armando and Susana's landlords gave them a farewell dinner the night before they left for Brazil.

Armando's and Susana's "cooling off" period turned out to be precisely that. It was the first week in September when the two arrived at a small coastal town in southern Brazil with the cover story that they were taking a brief vacation. Armando relates their experience:

The taxi driver who brought us from the airport told us we weren't going to like it much.

"The beach is beautiful when the sun is shining," he said, "but there's nobody there now. You've come at a bad time."

We arrived in the dead of winter. It was raining, and we were the only tourists in town. Everything was closed tight; not even the hotel was open. In that region there are several weeks of rain a year when it turns cold, and we arrived on the first day of winter.

The worst thing was that we couldn't go anywhere else, because we had a preestablished meeting set up nearby. We stayed in a small apartment overlooking the beach. Even the restaurants were closed. The only place in town that was open was a small grocery store where we bought our basic food supplies. The woman who rented the apartment lived in the same building and couldn't understand what was going on.

She must have thought I was a married man with money who had hooked up with a girl and brought her to this nothing town to spend a week or so. I told her I loved the ocean, and I'd go to the beach every day whether it was raining or not, with the wind chilling my bones. I'd run up and down, and I'd go into the water and come back to the apartment frozen stiff.

Susana adds:

We were alone in this apartment overlooking the ocean. I'd sit there, all bundled up, watching it rain. There wasn't a soul in sight, nor a car, nor even a bird. Nothing.

Everything was closed: hotels, restaurants, banks. It was so dead without the tourist trade that nothing functioned. There were a few permanent residents and a grocery store. They sold us the indispensable provisions, and we had nothing to do. After five days we traveled to a nearby town for an operational meeting, and nobody showed up. We waited two days more and returned for the fallback meeting. This time Julia showed up.

Ramón drove Julia to the Asunción airport to catch a plane for Brazil where she was to make her planned contact with Armando and Susana. As they drew into the parking area, Julia nudged Ramón's arm.

"Look," she said. "There are the cars."

Somoza's white Mercedes limousine and the red Ford Falcon were cruising slowly around the circumference of the parking lot with the four bodyguards inside the Falcon. Somoza was not in the Mercedes.

"He's coming back today," Ramón decided. "The morning plane from Buenos Aires is due in an hour."

The two of them deduced that during Somoza's agonizing disappearance for twenty days, he must have been undergoing a lengthy medical checkup in Buenos Aires.

"Bring Armando and Susana back with you, and fast," were Ramón's final words to Julia as he bade her good-bye at the departure gate.

> I was going to advise Armando and Susana to stay on longer, Julia recalls, but when we saw the two cars at the airport everything changed. I arrived at the meeting just on time. I couldn't even register at a hotel and leave my bags. It's not exactly normal to walk into an elegant restaurant carrying a suitcase, but I did it.
>
> Armando recommended special dishes.
>
> "Try this," he told me, "it's fantastic."
>
> Afterwards, I accompanied them to their apartment on the beach. The climate was awful, and Susana said everyone thought the two of them were crazy. They took me walking along the beach, and I nearly died from the cold.

Julia spent the night with Armando and Susana, and the following morning the three of them flew to Iguazú and crossed the border to the Paraguayan side of the falls. Julia returned to Asunción alone, while Armando and Susana rented an automobile and then registered at a hotel in the border city of Presidente Stroessner. That afternoon Susana visited a beauty salon to repair the damage wrought by the windblown salt during their Brazilian vacation. It was a unisex establishment, and there was a selection of men's and women's wigs on display. Susana's lips pursed thoughtfully as she studied a rugged, he-man wig.

"Just Armando's type," she told herself, "and we'll have to be disguised when we return to Asunción." She walked out of the shop with her hair feeling clean and light against her neck, carrying Armando's wig in a plain brown-paper package.

In Asunción, Ramón was convinced that the ex-dictator had returned, and he placed Osvaldo on the alert, but during the next several days Somoza remained invisible.

Julia telephoned the owner of the operational house to say she had come from Buenos Aires to contract the electricians who, within a few days, would start their work in the house.

CHAPTER 15

Ana had left Asunción for a large Brazilian city shortly after preparing the false documentation that enabled Julia to rent the operational base. She still had a key role to play in Santiago's getaway, but meanwhile her presence was not required in Paraguay. She took a room in an unpretentious hotel and lived quietly, occupying herself with reading and listening to all the news broadcasts she could pick up on her miniature transistor radio.

Ramón felt uneasy about the temporary apartment he and Julia had rented after Armando and Susana closed down their safe house. The landlady, he felt, was much too nosy. They had paid the first week's rent in advance, but when that term expired the two of them packed and left after Ramón explained that they had to cut short their vacation because he had been unexpectedly called back to his office in Buenos Aires.

Osvaldo's stand was flourishing, and he decided with a wry smile that, when he next talked business with the kiosk's owner, he would demand at least one-third of the profits from the enterprise.

Armando and Susana set out from Presidente Stroessner the morning after their arrival. They had to be in Asunción by mid-afternoon for an operational rendezvous at Santiago's house. At Susana's insistence, Armando was wearing his new wig, and he didn't like it. The skullcap effect over his thinning hair made his scalp feel hot and itchy, and when he absentmindedly scratched the itch, the wig went askew. He straightened it out with one hand, keeping the other on the steering wheel, and asked Susana if it was all right. She assured him that it was.

Armando was also dissatisfied with the automobile he had rented the previous afternoon. Before he had driven five kilometers he realized it was approaching the end of its useful life as a rental car. The motor was sluggish and needed a tune-up, the suspension was bad, and there was play in the steering gear. He promised himself he would exchange it that evening when they returned to Presidente Stroessner. They stopped for lunch at a restaurant in Coronel Oviedo, and as Armando got out of the car his head grazed the door frame and cocked the wig at a saucy angle over his right eyebrow.

"Straighten it out, Armando," Susana giggled. "You look ridiculous."

Armando snorted through his nostrils but held his temper as he climbed back into the car and used the rear view mirror to adjust the hairpiece. In the restaurant, he chose a table in the far corner, and as he studied the menu he murmured to his companion, "Look at them, Susana. They're nudging each other and pointing at me."

"Don't be silly, Armando. You're just feeling self-conscious, that's all."

The distance between Presidente Stroessner and Asunción is 330 kilometers, and they drove in silence. After all the months of forced togetherness, there was nothing left to talk about, and both of them were wound tight with the awareness that the climax of the operation was at last drawing near. There was also the nagging worry that, despite Armando's wig and Susana's dark glasses and new hairdo, they might be recognized on the streets of Asunción by one of their former acquaintances. In case that happened, they prepared the story that Armando had left the Peugeot on consignment at the used car lot and he was now returning to pick up the final payment.

The meeting at Santiago's house increased the burden of tension. They learned that Somoza had returned and Ramón had decided that the commando team would move in to occupy the operational base on Monday, September 15. Until then, the danger of Armando and Susana being recognized was too great to permit their remaining in Asunción. They might as well keep their hotel room in the border town and travel to the capital once a day to maintain contact with the rest of the team.

"I know it's going to be hard," Ramón told them," but it's better if you two stay on the move during these days. Anyone checking into a hotel during this coming period is automatically going to fall under suspicion. And if I were you, Armando, I'd do something about that wig. It doesn't look natural."

Armando and Susana stopped at a supermarket after leaving the meeting and laid in supplies for picnic lunches during the long-distance ordeals they faced over the next days. As Armando left the store carrying the box of groceries, a group of street urchins on the corner started hooting at him, and one of them cupped his hands to his lips and shouted, "Buy a wig."

Seething inside, Armando deposited the box in the back of the car. The next stop was at a gas station to fill the tank for the return trip to Presidente Stroessner. Armando's fists clench in exasperation at the memory of his ultimate humiliation:

> All day long the wig was snagging on things, slipping to one side or another, messing up my hair, and I put up with everything. On our return, I got out of the car at the gas station, and as the attendant filled the tank he kept staring at my head. I wanted to pay him, and he didn't look at the money; he had his eyes fixed on my head. I got back into the car, furious, and said to Susana, "Did you see that? We're drawing much more attention this way than without the damn wig."
>
> I pulled it off, threw it into the back of the car and didn't wear it again until the day of the operation.

Armando and Susana were mismatched, there was no doubt about it. In the original planning, Ramón had intended to match Armando with Ana and Susana with Santiago, but that team plan had to be changed when Ana broke her ankle.

Julia recalls:

You had to know the two of them to get the full flavor. They were a very special couple from every point of view. Armando's way of being was a total contrast with Susana's. To see the two of them on the streets of Asunción, with Armando wearing his wig, was incredible. I nearly died laughing.

They were totally different and Susana was unhappy about their being teamed up from the beginning. As revolutionaries we all respect each other, and I know that the two of them liked each other, but they had different criteria for solving certain practical problems. They added spice to our lives in Asunción. If they had to go out together, Susana worried about what shirt Armando should wear.

He is a very open, one-of-a-kind, person, and he's incapable of dissimulation. Susana, by way of contrast, was born for the clandestine life. She is very measured and knows how to keep her composure and live her cover. It was inevitable that the two of them would enter into contradictions.

Susana recalls:

I got along very badly with Armando. Terribly. As time went by I began to get over it. I began evaluating his qualities as a revolutionary militant, and I began to realize I shouldn't take such a hypercritical attitude towards him. I behaved intolerably toward Armando at times; not toward the others, just him. We shared too many things, too many tensions, for too long a time. I was with him during all those four long months in Paraguay.

Armando was the happiest person in the group. He loves dancing, music, food, parties. He is terribly emotional, and he weeps easily, without any complexes, without any restraint. He is free, the freest of us all. Something made him that way, totally free of hang-ups. When he is moved, he weeps, and he tells you freely what triggered the emotion.

Thus it was that the ill-matched couple began their ordeal of yo-yoing back and forth between Presidente Stroessner and Asunción during the final tense period of the operation.

Armando remembers:

We were staying in a hotel on the border. We drove to Asunción every day to make contact with Ramón and Santiago and find out what was happening. We traveled constantly during an entire week, 330 kilometers going and 330 kilometers returning each day. I have a lot of resistance when it comes to driving; I can drive for twenty hours without a rest, but this was too much. I was dead tired, and I'd fall asleep on my feet.

Susana picks up the thread:

We had no place to stay, and we were traveling all the time. It was insane, coming and going, coming and going. We went back to the hotel to sleep, and in the morning we left again. We'd see the *compañeros* for an operational meeting, we'd eat in a restaurant or look for a spot in the country to have a picnic. We'd visit one small town or another, and then we'd return. Sometimes we'd stop along the road and linger over a coke or a cup of coffee. We were totally exhausted when we got back to the hotel. My waist hurt from the long hours in the car. We took turns driving, but Armando bore the brunt of it. At the hotel, we always paid for the day in advance before we left, until the time came when we didn't return. We stayed in Asunción and rented a different sort of place.

It was September 10, 1980, the third day of Armando's and Susana's interminable Calvary. Osvaldo, seated in the kiosk on Avenida España, was galvanized against surprise. He stood up, reached for a magazine and began leafing through the pages slowly while from underneath his eyebrows, his dark, penetrating eyes followed the blue Mercedes that was approaching the kiosk, followed by the red Falcon. There he was, as haughty as ever, sitting beside the limousine's chauffeur. After twenty-one days of absence, Anastasio Somoza Debayle's return to Asunción was confirmed.

There was one final detail of great importance that had to be resolved: the selection and purchase of the vehicle that would be used in the operation and as a getaway car. It was at this point, Ramón and the others agreed, that a series of small complications began accumulating that were to lead to a fatal outcome.

It was decided that the vehicle should be a large pickup truck and that Armando would be the driver. Once the operation had been carried out, Ramón would climb into the cab with Armando while Santiago climbed into the back where he would have an open field of fire to cover their retreat.

Osvaldo was designated to buy the vehicle, inasmuch as his getaway plan was the simplest and fastest of all of them. Since Osvaldo worked all day in the news-stand and frequently until 10:00 at night, and since he was not an automobile expert to start with, it was left to Santiago to select the vehicle. Santiago, who was over six feet tall with red hair and beard, cut an unmistakable figure.

During the second week of September, Santiago chose the vehicle and told Osvaldo where he should go and which pickup he was to buy. The following day, Osvaldo left his assistant in charge of the kiosk and went to make the purchase. The pickup truck Santiago selected had just been sold to someone else. Osvaldo contacted Santiago, who in turn reported this development to Ramón.

> I told Santiago that the operation could be postponed or even fail for other reasons, but not for this. We had to guarantee all the material elements, and the pickup truck had to be available by Monday to transfer the arms to the operational base and set the operation in motion. And by Monday we had the truck.

In order to make the purchase, Santiago had to return to the used car lot the following morning, make a hasty selection, and send Osvaldo off to buy the pickup a few hours later. Although they never appeared together, the owner of the lot connected them mentally and afterwards was able to give a description of both of them to the police.

During the weekend, Ramón and Santiago repainted the truck in the latter's garage, but they were unable to locate in any of the Asunción hardware stores the proper type of Carborundum steel file to remove the serial numbers of the motor and chassis and thus delay identification of the vehicle. The motor had turned over promptly when Santiago tested it on the lot, but during the weekend they discovered that it was difficult to start when the motor was cold. It was too late to rectify the mistake; this was the vehicle they had to use.

Ramón and Julia had moved to a hotel the previous week. Osvaldo left the boarding house and moved in with Santiago. Armando and Susana faced a thorny security problem that they still had not resolved by the night of Sunday, September 14. The vigil was to begin the following morning at 6:00 a.m. and would continue daily until the target appeared and the trap was sprung. To rent a hotel room in Asunción at this point, only to abandon it moments after the operation, was impossible, as it would give the police a clear lead. That night, as they had done for the past week, they returned to their hotel room in Presidente Stroessner, more than 300 kilometers from the operational area.

CHAPTER 16

Armando arose at 5 a.m. on Monday, September 15, and tiptoed through the hotel lobby so as not to awaken the night clerk. There wasn't a soul on the streets of Presidente Stroessner as he set off on his long journey. The rental car he was driving was in good condition, and he held it at a steady 120 kilometers per hour on the straight, flat highway. But that was the only plus factor, he thought gloomily. Susana would remain in the hotel room all day long, and he himself would not reappear at the hotel until after 9:00 p.m. What a pattern for a pair of Argentine honeymooners who, presumably, had spent each day of the past week overwhelmed by the natural beauties of Iguazú falls.

The previous day, at Ramón's suggestion, he had tried to rent one of the small, back-alley apartments in Asunción that are available on a daily rental basis, but it was a Sunday and the landlady had not been at home. He would have to make the arrangement this evening, after they closed down their day-long vigil.

In Asunción, Ramón appeared at Santiago's house at 5:30 a.m. He changed into workmen's overalls identical to those Santiago was wearing, and the two of them removed the back of the sofa, took out the weapons and placed them in their original wooden crates, nailing down the covers. They lifted the crates into the back of the Chevrolet pickup truck and, while Ramón opened the garage doors, Santiago turned over the motor. It balked as usual when the engine was cold, but finally caught on the fourth or fifth try, and Santiago backed out of the garage, nursing the throttle, while Ramón closed and locked the garage doors and climbed into the cab beside him. Osvaldo, with one of the pair of walkie-talkies concealed in the inner pocket of his jacket, had already left the house to open the kiosk.

Shortly after 6:00 a.m., Santiago backed the pickup into the garage of the operational base on Avenida España. Ramón closed the garage doors, and the two of them removed the arms crates from the truck, carried them into the semi-furnished living room, and pried the lids off the boxes.

Armando had made one brief stop alongside the deserted highway to change into workmen's overalls similar to those worn by Santiago and Ramón. He parked his car at the prearranged rendezvous point bordering the Asunción cemetery and walked the several blocks to the operational house. It was 8 a.m. sharp when he appeared. The weapons had been inspected and loaded, and the vigil began.

Armando's weapon was a FAL combat rifle. He checked the clip and levered a round into the chamber. He entered the garage, tucked the FAL into the right angle formed by the wide seat and the backrest, climbed into the seat and rehearsed the motions of braking the car, shifting to neutral, setting the hand brake, flinging the door open and swiveling out of the car with the FAL swinging up to firing position.

Ramón was at his observation post next to the living room window; the walkie-talkie, its receiver switch on, hissed and crackled on the coffee table at his side. His M-16 combat rifle, with thirty bullets in the clip, lay across the table, and he also carried a Browning 9mm. pistol in one of his capacious overall pockets. Santiago's weapon, the RPG-2 bazooka, was propped beside the front door, along with the two Ingram submachine guns, both fitted with silencers.

The three members of the commando team had long since memorized the operational plan of action. Julia had provided them with an accurate sketch of the downstairs interior of the house and the location of the connecting door to the garage. They also had a scale map of the house, front yard, and the stretch of Avenida España fronting the house and had rehearsed Armando's maneuvers in the Chevrolet, using matchboxes to represent the pickup truck and Somoza's two-car convoy. Now for the first time the three of them were on location, verifying that the plan was feasible. Ramón had only a few points to review.

"Osvaldo's signal to us will be the color of the car Somoza is using, repeated three times. I've been out in the front yard timing the traffic this morning, and it takes from twenty-three to twenty-nine seconds for an automobile to reach here after passing Osvaldo's news stand, so we all have to be in our places within twenty seconds after we hear the signal."

Ramón tensed and held up a warning hand as a figure turned in at the gate and approached the front door.

"Hide the weapons," he hissed. Santiago scooped up the bazooka and the two Ingrams, while Armando swept the M-16 and walkie-talkie off the table, and the two of them disappeared through the open door into the garage.

Ramón waited for the doorbell to ring a second time before opening it. The caller was a young man in workman's attire.

"I'm the watchman here," he introduced himself, "and the young lady said I should come here today to collect my pay."

"That's right," Ramón nodded, "she told me about you. She's going to be here at 12:00 noon, so please come back then."

The other two returned to the room and replaced the weapons in their ready positions as the caller walked away. Ramón glanced at his watch.

"Osvaldo is going to call in at 9:00 sharp to test the walkie-talkie. Meanwhile, we can run through the exercise, without arms, naturally. Blue, blue, blue."

Ramón strode out the front door and took up his position near the low wall that separated the front lawn from the sidewalk. Santiago simulated picking up the bazooka and waited inside the front door until Ramón gave him the signal to advance. Armando rushed into the garage, flung the doors wide open, climbed into the cab, and started swearing steadily as the starter motor ground over and over and the motor refused to catch.

"A disaster!" was Ramón's only comment when he entered the garage and pulled the doors closed behind him. "What's wrong with it, Gordo?"

Armando finally got the motor started on the third, lengthy

try and revved the engine up, then let it idle while he listened critically.

"Probably burnt-out valves and poor compression," he said. "Let me check it out."

He pulled the hood release lever, got out, raised the hood, and started pulling off the sparkplug cables one by one. Ramón walked back into the house, sat down again by the front window and waited for Osvaldo's test call.

At 9:00 a.m. on the dot—Ramón had his eyes on the second hand of his watch—there was an alteration in the noise level of the walkie-talkie, an increased burst of static and a wholly-blurred sequence of words. The noise level dropped back to a slight hissing as Ramón frowned at the apparatus. It must have been Osvaldo broadcasting on the agreed schedule, but the signal wasn't getting through. The team had tested the two walkie-talkies dozens of times during the past months, and usually over distances considerably greater than that separating the kiosk from the operational base. Osvaldo, along with the others, had demonstrated time and again his ability to handle the transceiver. The batteries in both radios were fresh. Ramón picked up the walkie-talkie and pressed the transmit button. "One zero one, we don't receive you. Over."

Again there was an increased burst of static and an indistinguishable reply. Santiago was leaning over Ramón's shoulder, listening anxiously.

"He's not getting through to us, Flaco. You'll have to go up there, make sure he broadcast to us on schedule and find out if he heard our message and replied. Take new batteries with you, check the contact points for dust or corrosion and call me again at 9:20. Your message will be: 'Three zero three, three zero three, over.' If I receive you, I'll reply immediately."

Santiago nodded, went to the garage and took two plastic-wrapped batteries out of the toolkit resting on the Chevrolet's broad fender.

"How's it going, Armando?"

Armando shrugged.

"I'm cleaning the points. We'll see if that helps."

Santiago disappeared, and Ramón resumed his waiting.

At 9:20, Santiago's voice came through, loud and clear.

"Three zero three, three zero three, over."

Ramón exhaled with relief and pressed the Transmit button.

"Three zero three here. Receiving you loud and clear. Out."

Santiago returned ten minutes later and reported, "Osvaldo broadcast on schedule at 9:00. He received your message and responded to it. The set was in good working order, and the batteries appeared to be okay, but I changed them anyway. Then I called you and received your answer. And just to make sure it's working now, I told Osvaldo to give us a call at 9:45 sharp."

Armando appeared from the garage, with rolled-up sleeves and grease-stained hands.

"How is the pickup doing?" Ramón asked him.

"I did what I could, but it's a crock of shit. The valves are burnt out. The best we can do is to warm up the motor every hour so it will turn over when we need it."

Armando went off to scrub his hands, and at 9:45 all three were gathered around the walkie-talkie. Once again there was a change in the background level, and with difficulty they caught the words, "...zero three, three zero..."

"It's something about his location," Ramón decided. "Exactly where were you standing when you broadcast the message to us, Flaco?"

"Let's see. After we'd talked about the problem and checked our watches to make sure they were synchronized, I took the set from him, tucked it inside my overall and went into the men's room just inside the bowling alley to check out the contacts and change the batteries. I came back out, looked around to make sure I wasn't being observed, turned my face away from the street and put through the call to you."

"So you were about 15 feet away from the kiosk?"

Santiago nodded, then clapped his forehead.

"Of course!" he said, "it has to be the cables. There are high tension cables running directly above the news-stand. They must be damping out his signal."

"Right. Go back up there and tell him about it. When he sights

the target, he'll have to leave the kiosk and walk toward the
bowling alley entrance when he transmits. Have him do that and
put through another call at 10:15. I'll respond to it."

The 10:15 call was successful. Osvaldo's voice was distinct, and
Armando clapped Ramón on the back with relief at having
surmounted another obstacle.

Julia visited the Korean supermarket at 9:30 on Monday and
bought the fixings for the commando team's lunch. As she passed
Osvaldo's news-stand with her shopping bag, she recognized
Santiago—despite his disguise—talking to Osvaldo, and she
wondered uneasily what problem had arisen. She arrived at the
operational house before Santiago returned and joined the vigil for
two hours while she prepared ham and cheese sandwiches and
opened bottles of Coca Cola for the three of them and herself. Had
the operation taken place during her visit to the house, she would
have joined in with one of the Ingram submachine guns to lay
down covering fire against Somoza's bodyguards.

The watchman arrived promptly at noon. Julia paid him for
his two weeks' work and told him his presence would no longer be
required as the house would be occupied from then on. The
watchman was later to provide Julia's and Ramón's description to
the police.

Julia left the house shortly after noon, and the vigil continued
until 6 p.m. when gathering dusk made clear-cut identification
difficult. It had been agreed from the very beginning that the
operation must be carried out during daylight hours and the
target's presence in the limousine must be unmistakably verified
before the action could start.

Armando stopped in a residential area of Asunción and negotiated
the rental on a daily basis of half of a duplex apartment behind
one of the houses. He paid five days rent in advance and told the
landlady that he and his wife would be moving in late that same
evening.

Susana explains why this was the perfect solution to their
security problem:

The apartment was totally independent with its own entrance. We didn't see another soul there. The only one who saw the owner was Armando when he paid several days' rent in advance and received the key from her. It was a duplex apartment that a married couple rented on a semi-secret basis. They didn't pay taxes on their profits, they didn't give us a receipt, they didn't bother us. All we had to do was pay in advance, and no record was kept of the transaction.

Armando drove to Presidente Stroessner, picked up Susana and their bags and checked out of the hotel there. They ate dinner in the border town and afterwards drove back to their new refuge. Armando, more exhausted than ever after covering 1,000 kilometers in a single day, plus putting in a tense ten-hour vigil at the operational house, climbed into bed shortly after midnight and started snoring the moment his head hit the pillow.

CHAPTER 17

Armando arose, well-rested for the first time in days, on Tuesday morning, September 16, 1980, and departed for the operational house at 7:40. He caught a taxi to a point four blocks away from his destination and walked the remaining distance. He carried no identification with him; none of the members of the commando team did. Susana had Armando's billfold and passport; Julia had Ramón's; Santiago left his papers in his safe-house, since he had to return there after the operation. Osvaldo's papers were tucked into the Adidas bag, along with all his other possessions, and the bag rested on the floor in the rear of Santiago's car.

At 7:55, Susana left the daily-rental apartment with the couple's two suitcases, placed them in the trunk of the car and drove to Position A: the parking lot of a shopping center.

> There I could wait for a reasonable length of time, but not all day. I had told Armando: "I can wait for you here until 1 p.m. At 1 p.m. I will go to Position B and wait for you there until 6:00."
>
> Sometimes I stayed in the car, sometimes I got out, but I had to be there, close to the car. I spent hours sitting in the car, reading, waiting for Armando to turn up.

Julia remained in her hotel room after Ramón left for "work" that morning. Their rented car was parked in the garage in the basement of the hotel. Ana, of course, was far away in a hotel room in Brazil, listening to the hourly news broadcasts on her radio.

Osvaldo's transmitting problems with the walkie-talkie had

been resolved the previous day, and at 8:15 he left the kiosk, walked toward the bowling alley, pressed down on the transmit button and spoke into his jacket lapel, "Three zero three, three zero three, over."

Ramón's metallic voice came back a few seconds later, "This is three zero three. We're receiving you well. Out."

The three commando members were in their places as the second day's vigil began, and the communications system, on which everything depended, was working perfectly. Or so they thought.

We were all sitting there, Armando recalls, in a silence in which you could hear a fly buzzing. Suddenly we heard, "Hello, hello, hello," and we started running to our places, thinking it was Osvaldo. The first time, I climbed into the pickup and started the motor until Ramón told me, "It's not him."

It was a commercial company broadcasting on our frequency. Apparently, it was a highway construction company communi-cating with its transportation units. This happened three times on Tuesday, and it certainly didn't help the tension.

We spent all Tuesday waiting, with a few false alarms. Santiago was in the front of the house with his bazooka and submachine gun ready to go. I had the pickup in the garage with the driver's door open. I turned the motor over every hour so it wouldn't balk when we needed it. I had the FAL on the seat, and I was carrying a pistol. Ramón spent most of the time at the dining room table, listening to the walkie-talkie. We tried not to go to the bathroom unless we absolutely had to. We literally didn't want to be caught with our pants down when the signal came through. At midday we ate cold meat sandwiches, drank a glass of water, took turns going to the bathroom, and went back to our alert positions. That's how we spent all day Monday and Tuesday.

I was exhausted when I got back to the apartment. Before we left the operational house, Santiago had told me, "You'll see; it's going to happen tomorrow between 10:00 a.m. and 12:00."

I told Susana about this, and she said, "I also have the hunch that it's going to be tomorrow."

We went shopping on Tuesday evening, Susana remembers, and Armando said, "Today we hardly had anything to eat for lunch. I don't want that to happen again tomorrow."

He bought a minced ham and olive roll that looked delicious, and a loaf of bread. He was very happy with his big olive roll, and he put it in the refrigerator when we got back to the apartment.

"Don't worry," I told him, "you're never going to eat that, because the operation is going to come off before noon tomorrow. It'll probably happen around 10 in the morning, because on Wednesday that's the time he passes by."

Somoza had only passed by on that day and time once before, and I don't know why it occurred to me that he might repeat the pattern.

"Why do you say that?" Armando asked me.

"I suppose it's because Wednesday is in the middle of the week. Monday no, because he still has a hangover from the weekend, and for types like him, the weekend starts on Thursday. I just feel that Wednesday is our best bet."

These are the sort of things one says, and of course there's no logic to them. They're simply expressions of desire.

On Wednesday I gave Armando a good-bye kiss and told him, "Lots of luck, brother, because today's the day. I'll be waiting for you before noon."

Early on Wednesday—Armando picks up the thread—I caught a cab and then walked a few blocks to the operational house. It was a chilly morning, and I was in shirt-sleeves. I had my wig on and a bag with the bread and luncheon meat under my arm. People were looking at me as if I were crazy.

When I arrived and unpacked the bag, Ramón said, "We aren't going to have a chance to eat that this noon."

We took up our positions, tested the walkie-talkie, and warmed-up the pickup's motor as we did each morning, and settled down to wait. Osvaldo only had to transmit the color of the car he was riding in. There's an interesting detail here: for several seconds, Somoza's life hung on a newspaper.

Osvaldo tells the story as follows:

I was at the news-stand, chatting with someone who always
brought me *empanadas*. It was around 10:00 a.m., and I was
sitting down when I saw Somoza's car coming. I stood up to
get a good look. I recognized the license plate, but when I
looked inside I couldn't make out anything. Or to be more
accurate, I saw a man in the back seat reading a newspaper
and another man sitting beside him. Another thing that
confused me was that Somoza always sat in the front seat
beside the driver. When he was only ten or fifteen meters
away he lowered the paper and I identified him.

I told this other kid I had to take a shit, and I headed for
the bathroom. I stepped inside the bowling alley and
transmitted the signal: "White, white, white."

I hadn't noticed that there was a man inside the lobby,
painting. I repeated the signal, and he looked at me as if I
were crazy. He was painting over a poster with white paint,
and he must have thought I was commenting on his work. I
was wearing my windbreaker with my hand in the pocket
pressing the transmit button. I repeated the message a third
time and then went into the bathroom inside the bowling
alley and came out expecting to hear the sound of shooting,
but I didn't hear a thing. I looked at my watch.

It was 10:05 in the morning of Wednesday, September 17,
1980. Julio César Gallardo, Somoza's longtime chauffeur and
bodyguard, was at the wheel of the Mercedes. In the rear, sitting
next to the ex-dictator, was Joseph Bainitin, his North American
economic adviser.

Armando told us:

If God exists, he must be a *guerrillero*, because of all the tests
we made, this one came through the clearest of all. I opened
the door of the pickup, got in, turned the motor over, and
pulled out to the sidewalk. There was the white Mercedes
pulled up at the stop light about sixty meters away. I reversed,
pulled back nearly into the garage and waited for him to come
to us.

Ramón then told us:

I went into the garden and saw the car sixty meters away,
while Armando was at the wheel of the pickup ready to cut
off the traffic. With practice, we had cut our time of getting
into position to thirteen seconds after we heard the signal. I
had a reference point: when the front of the car coincided
with a certain tree I gave Santiago a signal, so he wouldn't
come out earlier and let someone see him with the bazooka.
Armando was awaiting my signal to head into the street and
block traffic.

Armando continued:

I saw Ramón waiting to give Santiago the signal to get into
firing position, and the truth is I didn't look at him after that.
He was supposed to signal me when to pull out, but I was
watching Somoza's car and, as a professional, I knew exactly
when I had to make my move and how many cars I had to
cut off. When I saw that the limousine had started up with
five or six cars ahead of it, I let most of them go past and
then I pulled out in the pickup and aimed straight for a
Volkswagen Combi that was in front of the Somoza car. The
driver slammed on the brakes and swerved into the middle
of the street. As I set the brake and climbed out, I heard the
first shots: "Bam, bam, bam."

In accordance with the preestablished plan, Santiago had to
take the first shot with the bazooka in case the limousine was
bullet-proof. Ramón, from the front garden, watched the
limousine pass in front of the marker tree and gave Santiago the
signal to take up his attack position. When Armando blocked the
Volkswagen van, the dictator's car braked. Ramón heard a noise
behind him and turned to see Santiago on one knee, struggling
with the bazooka. Thinking the latter had slipped and fallen, he
swiveled, raised the M-16 to his shoulder and started squeezing off
shots.

What had really happened was that the first bazooka charge

was a dud. When a bazooka misfires, one is supposed to wait thirty seconds before removing the defective projectile and replacing it with another. Santiago didn't wait even two seconds. He knelt, pulled the projectile out of the mouth of the tube and replaced it with the spare. He got to his feet again and took aim but didn't fire. The Somoza limousine, its driver already dead, drifted aimlessly toward the operational house and ran into the curb exactly in front of Ramón, who kept firing methodically into the back seat. The limousine was not bullet-proof, and each of the shots penetrated the car through the shattered back window. Ramón was so close to the Mercedes that a bazooka round at that moment would have killed him.

Ramón continues his account:

I started firing single rounds, first at the driver who had already braked. The car kept drifting and came to a stop just in front of the door. I shifted my aim to the other two. Somoza never knew what hit him, he was staring straight ahead.

It wasn't until then that Somoza's bodyguards went into action. I hadn't so much as seen them. When I wanted to start firing at them, I discovered the M-16 was empty. Santiago had withdrawn into the entrance and was ready to fire. I ran over to where he was and said, "Give it to him now."

He fired from inside the house. The explosion was tremendous. We could see that the auto was totally destroyed. The bodyguards were hiding behind the wall of the next door house. They had stopped firing.

The pickup's motor stalled, Armando continued, and I climbed back in. The van I had cut off was backing and filling the street. The driver was desperate. I started the motor, and when I got out again, *Bam!*—a deafening explosion. The Volkswagen cramped its wheels, found an opening and took off like a scalded cat. The explosion left me shaking.

With the Volkswagen out of the way, I could see the Somoza car blown apart, metal scraps and shattered glass all over the street. I was blocking the avenue in front of the house.

Our getaway route was via a street turning off to the left about ten meters beyond the operational house. The cars coming the other way were backing up and turning around. I had to cut off the getaway street before any of them could block it, so I got back in the pickup and pulled ahead ten meters to cut off the street. When I got out again, I heard shots and I saw the bodyguards behind the wall of the next-door house, and one of them was firing at Santiago and Ramón. Flaco was behind the front door, firing the submachine gun that made no noise because it was fitted with a silencer. I brought the FAL up and shot at one of them. I don't think I hit him, but he dropped to the ground. I shouted to Santiago, "Come on, I'll cover you."

One of the guards raised his head to see what was going on, and I fired again. Pieces of the wall flew in all directions. Ramón came running and climbed into the cab. I let go four or five more rounds so they'd keep their heads down. I remember I said to Ramón, "We blew him away."

"Yeah," he replied, "he won't bother anybody any more."

Flaco came running toward us, and I shifted into first and took off. The pickup was already moving when he jumped into the back.

I turned into the getaway street, accelerated and thirty meters down that street, pah, pah, pah, the motor died on me.

"This piece of shit has had it," I told Ramón. "Let's get ourselves another car."

Just then, a little Mitsubishi came down the street toward us. Ramón said, "Okay, let's take this one."

We got on both sides of it, and the driver slammed on the brakes and raised his hands. I opened the door and said, "Get out, or I'll blow your head off."

"Sure, sure," he said, and he went scurrying off.

This took about two seconds. The three of us climbed in, and we took off. We could barely squeeze into the car.

CHAPTER 18

The balky Chevrolet pickup remained stalled in the middle of the getaway street with the arms scattered in the cab and the back. The license plates had been removed and hidden to delay identification, but the telltale engine and chassis serial numbers had not been effaced. The original plan had been to take part of the arms along during the getaway and hide them in a third cache, but there was no room for them in the tiny Mitsubishi, and they had to be abandoned.

Armando's first stop was at the Asunción cemetery to let Santiago off at the point where his car was parked, since Santiago's first responsibility was to help Osvaldo make his escape from Paraguay.

Osvaldo told us:

I came out of the bowling alley and saw that the painter was still at it. The kid who brought me *empanadas* didn't say anything; he just kept on reading his magazine. I went out into the street and saw Somoza's car against the curb. The top part of it was black, and there were people gathering around it. I told the kid I had a bad stomach and I was going home.

"I'm going to close up," I told him. "Take the magazine."

I'd already cleaned the stand, and now I padlocked it. I crossed over to the gas station. There was another kid on a bicycle who said to me, "You know what happened? A car blew up."

"Where?" I asked.

"Just down the street. Come on, let's go."

"No," I said, "I have a bad stomach."

"I'll take you," he said.

"No," I told him. "I'm in a hurry; I have to get home."

I turned down the other street toward the cemetery, which was two-and-a-half blocks away. I had to meet Santiago there. I waited a few minutes for him, and we climbed into his car and left. When we first met by the cemetery, I asked him how everything had gone.

"We blew him away," he told me, "but there were problems."

"What kind of problems?"

I was afraid one of the team had been wounded.

"The pickup stalled and we had to leave it. We took a Mitsubishi, and we had to change the getaway route."

I had to change clothes as we drove. Santiago knew what my escape route was.

"Throw your jacket out here," he told me.

I tossed it out the window, and strangely enough, it caught on a shrub and stayed hanging there as if to show that I had passed by. After that I started taking the walkie-talkie apart to throw the pieces out separately, but Santiago told me to throw the whole thing out the window. All I'd managed to do was strip the antenna off.

We turned on the radio and started listening, but there wasn't anything of interest. When we arrived at Italramada, the port, the first news flash was being broadcast, and five minutes later they were reporting that six blond Argentines had done the job.

Santiago had his escape route, and I had mine, but I told him, "Come with me."

We were listening to the news flashes, and Santiago told me, "Look, I'd like to go with you, Osvaldo. I don't know why we didn't arrange things that way."

"Then let's go," I said. "Grab your suitcase."

"No," he said, "I can't do it."

I didn't want to say anything more, because these were plans we'd been working on for months, and you can't change them on a moment's notice. We said good-bye there, and he added, "Take care of yourself, Osvaldo."

"No," I told him, "you take care. I'm on my way."

And I left him there in Italramada.

Armando's second stop was to let Ramón off a block away from the hotel where Julia was waiting. Julia, for her part, had had a feeling that the operation would be carried out on the previous day, Tuesday. When that didn't happen, she told us, she felt "a little bit let down":

> I thought, God knows how long we're going to be here. The hotel was relatively close to the scene of the operation, but I had heard nothing and felt nothing. I was half asleep and not even fully dressed, because I had told myself it wasn't going to happen today.
>
> When Ramón appeared, he told me, "We did it! We did it-t-t!"
>
> I couldn't believe it, and I asked, "Are you sure it was Somoza?"
>
> "Of course! I saw him clearly. And besides, if the M-16 didn't do the job, the bazooka certainly did."
>
> I saw he had a small wound on his hand where a bullet had nicked him. I cleaned it with a handkerchief and put a Band-Aid on it. Then we both changed in a hurry.
>
> Keeping your cool is what saves a person. It was past 10:00 in the morning, and Ramón told me, "Go have breakfast while I take care of the bill. Have something, even if it's only a glass of milk."
>
> I went to the coffee shop, and the milk felt like lead in my stomach. After that, we went to the hotel garage, got into the car and left.

I was in the parking lot of that shopping center, Susana recalls, with the radio held to my ear. I was seated behind the wheel, petrified, waiting for the news. The first flash came at about 10:10. They cut off the normal broadcast and announced: "A late news flash: an automobile was blown up."

I held my breath, and my heart was hammering.

"Dear God!" I said, "Get back here; let's get out of here; let's go!" Then they said something on the radio that I'll never forget, it was so ridiculous. They said, "Somebody fired a bomb at a white Mercedes-Benz."

That was incredible. I knew what had happened, but

the general public didn't. The news flashes kept coming, and at 10:15 I couldn't listen any longer; I was desperate.

Armando showed up at 10:20. I remember he had a huge smile on his face. He grabbed my hand and said, "We did it! We did it!"

We had spent so many months waiting for this moment that I was overwhelmed. I know Armando, and he was trembling. He told me, "Move over. I have to do the driving or I won't be able to handle this."

I let him take the wheel, but then I told him, "Change your clothes."

He changed out of the overalls right there, and we left. I started interrogating him.

"Did you drop Ramón off?"

"Of course."

"Was Osvaldo waiting for you, and did Santiago get off?"

"Yes, yes."

"Did you take the weapons?"

"We couldn't."

"Why not?"

"Because the pickup broke down."

I was bubbling over with questions, and Armando told me, "Cool down; we have to get out of here. Start watching the traffic."

I started watching what was moving around us and listening to the radio.

"Did everybody get away according to plan?"

"Yes."

"And nobody was wounded?"

"No."

"And you're positive it was him?"

"Absolutely, and there's nothing left."

Osvaldo continues the story of his escape:

There in Italramada I bought my ticket, and I got into the passenger launch. It wasn't due to leave until 10:50. Everybody and his brother was jabbering over the radio, saying they were Argentines, there were six of them, they were all blond, lots of stuff like that.

There was a kid there who was playing checkers, and I pretended to be watching him, but I was really listening to the radio. He beat his opponent and asked me, "Do you know how to play?"

"Sure," I told him.

"Sit down," he said, so I sat down and we started to play. I was concentrating on the news bulletins and moving the pieces without paying attention. He took four or five of my pieces and got a queen. We kept on playing, but I was listening to the radio and rehearsing my cover story, and he wiped me out. He offered me a chance to get even, but I said, "We don't have time; we're almost there."

We disembarked on the Argentine side of the river, and they were already talking about sending all of us back to Paraguay. Lots of the passengers were furious, grumbling among themselves. I arrived thinking I'd pass through easily. I didn't believe they'd be able to close all the borders as rapidly as they did and create the chaos of the next days.

They went through my bag in Customs. I had the radio/recorder Armando had given me and an umbrella I had bought in Asunción. The Customs officer told me, "This radio/recorder and this umbrella require duty."

"Fine," I said. "How much?"

The idiot started rifling through lists, and catalogs and papers. He didn't know how much to charge for that model. And he couldn't find the amount of duty on the umbrella either. He went into the office and left me sitting there. It had already been announced that Somoza was the one killed. The launch that set out from Argentina for Paraguay when we arrived was turned back. I was on the last boat that left Paraguay.

I told the Customs officer that he could keep the radio, no problem. What's one radio more or less? If I had known it was going to create a problem I wouldn't have bought it. By now, he was looking for a way out.

Finally he said, "No, no, here it is. The duty is so much."

I paid what he asked. I walked twenty or thirty meters down the street to the bus station, and at 1:00 p.m. I caught a bus for Formosa.

Ana told us:

I left Paraguay at the end of August, thinking that everything was ready and that the operation would take place within the next few days. Nobody knew that Somoza was going to disappear for three weeks. I was in Río, and I received a message from Ramón to wait there, because there was a delay. I was supposed to wait outside the country until the operation took place and then enter immediately, meet Santiago, and come back out with him. I was supposed to arrange Santiago's passport with the same seals that mine bore, so both of us could leave as if we had entered Paraguay one day after the operation. I arranged a meeting with Santiago for the day following the operation and for two fall-back meetings in case one of us didn't show up. We estimated that it would be difficult for them to close the borders, but that if they did, the closure couldn't last for more than one day.

I kept on waiting, listening to news broadcasts, reading the papers every day, until by the 17th of September I couldn't stand it any longer. When I heard on the radio that the operation had come off successfully, I reacted so strongly I didn't know what to do. I started jumping up and down, throwing my clothes into the suitcase and listening to the news bulletins. They told about finding the pickup truck with the arms in it, said the public reaction was one of surprise and in some sectors joyfulness. The Brazilian radio referred to Somoza as a dictator, and I remember one radio station said: "Somoza wasn't killed; he was removed from the planet."

I learned immediately that the border had been closed. I kept on listening and heard a broadcast from Nicaragua, declaring it a day of national jubilation and telling how the people were out in the streets celebrating.

When the news reached Nicaragua, work stopped as if by unanimous accord in all offices and factories, and people clustered around radios to hear the bulletins, minute by minute, giving the details of the operation. *Barricada*, the official newspaper, published an edition the following day with an enormous banner headline that read: "All Nicaragua a Sea of Joyfulness." The story began as follows:

The National Directorate of our revolutionary vanguard, The Sandinista National Liberation Front (FSLN), yesterday headed a gigantic demonstration along the principal streets and neighborhoods of the capital to join in the popular jubilation over the execution of former dictator Somoza.

The caravan and popular demonstration wound through the eastern sectors of town where fifteen months earlier thousands of Nicaraguans had died beneath the indiscriminate bombardment of Somoza's air force.

The National Directorate exhorted FSLN militants to "join in the popular rejoicing on this day of National Celebration." The mass concentration poured into the Plaza of the Revolution where the people celebrated the event with popular dances.

Comandante William Ramírez referred to the operation against Somoza as "an exemplary act, an act of justice and of true revolutionary internationalism." There were other spontaneous celebrations in León, Masaya, Chinandega, Carazo and Granada.

El Nuevo Diario said:

The news of the death of the most genocidal member of the Somoza dynasty ran through the capital like a gunpowder train. For some, the presence in any country on earth of the bloody-handed ex-dictator, was a serious threat to our tranquillity and peace. Only the physical disappearance of the genocidal tyrant could bring us relief."

In the Extra edition of *Barricada* on September 17th, the National Directorate of the FSLN issued the following communiqué:

To the heroic people of Nicaragua and to the world: The National Directorate of the FSLN, on confirming the bringing to justice of the genocidal Anastasio Somoza Debayle, joins in the national rejoicing of the people of Sandino who see fulfilled in this heroic action their desire for justice and popular vengeance against the man who massacred more than 100,000 Nicaraguans and submerged our country in misery and ignominy, the man who assassinated Pablo Leal, Báez Bone, Edwin Castro, Ajax Delgado, Casamiro Sotelo, Pedro Joaquín Chamorro and many other patriots, the man who ordered the genocide in Waslala, Sofana, Estelí, León, Monimbó, Chinandega, Matagalpa, Managua, Carazo and so many other martyred cities of Nicaragua.

The fighting spirit, the self-abnegation and bravery of the heroic commando team that executed the tyrant embodies the implacable will of the people of Rigoberto. In this spirit we will continue forging the homeland of Sandino.

Exactly fourteen months after having fled from revolutionary justice, and seven years after the dictator ordered the execution of our beloved brothers, Oscar Turcios and Ricardo Morales, Somoza has paid for his crimes.

Susana and Armando soon realized that President Stroessner had ordered the hugest manhunt in Paraguayan history. Not only that, but he had closed all the borders of his country as a feudal baron might padlock the gates to his castle so that no one could enter or leave. Armando remembers the first stage of their getaway as follows:

We were feeling very much alone amidst an incredible repression and a nationwide manhunt. We couldn't predict what might happen to us. Suddenly we heard a radio bulletin that said, "In Managua, the Governing Junta has issued a communiqué congratulating the heroic commando team for having imposed justice and for having made the dictator pay for all his infamies. "The people have taken over the streets and are celebrating. Today has been declared a Day of

National Jubilation."

When we heard about the celebration in Managua, Susana and I wept for two hours. It filled us with great strength and happiness, and we told each other, "Okay, no matter what happens to us now, we've completed our duty." And we wept, knowing that even if we died, we had made an entire people happy. It was a blow to the entire Latin American counter-revolution that a tyrant had paid in this way for his crimes. It was a day of happiness and rejoicing for the entire progressive world.

Susana recalls:

We went to Encarnación because we were Argentines returning home. We had driven about fifty kilometers when we encountered the first roadblock. They stopped us, searched the car, asked for our documents, asked us where we were coming from, what our business was, where we were going. Simple questions. For us, this was a piece of cake. I, personally, lived in Argentina until 1978, with the army stopping me five times a day in the street. We told them that we were bringing some Paraguayan hammocks back with us to sell in Argentina, which was a normal, everyday thing.

Thirty kilometers further on there was another roadblock, and there were about six more before we reached the border. When we got to Encarnación, we began to relax. We already knew that the border was closed, because during the trip they had announced that all the frontiers were closed and that no flights were allowed to enter or leave the country. We looked the situation over, listened to people commenting, saw the way people were bunching up in Encarnación and the paralysis. So we drove back a number of kilometers and went to a farm we had foreseen as a safe haven in case we needed one.

The owners were a Paraguayan couple we had befriended in Asunción, and we were welcome there. This is very common in that region. You pay for your stay as if you were in a hotel, so when we arrived they were happy to see us. We told them, "We're coming from Encarnación, and we don't know what is going on. Something is happening; they stopped us along the road. We think the border has been closed. We came in this morning and were shopping in Encarnación. We were planning to spend a few days with you, and we saw something strange was happening. As we left town, we were stopped by the police."

We turned on the radio. This farm couple knew nothing about what had happened, and we listened to the news bulletins together. Then, with the border closed, we didn't even have to ask them if we could stay with them. They were happy because they would earn a few pesos, and we were easy to get along with. As the days went by, they said, "The border is still closed, so you'll have to stay on with us."

And we said, "This is terrible, with all the work we have to do piling up back home."

Julia told us:

After leaving Asunción, we didn't even listen to the radio so we wouldn't get nervous. When the police stopped us the first time, Ramón asked, "Why are you stopping us?"

The policeman was upset and confused, and he told us, "Because they killed the president."

"*What!*" we exclaimed. "*The president?*"

"No, no. The president of Nicaragua."

They searched the car superficially and let us by.

We came to another roadblock, controlled by an arrogant youngster who gave us a hard time. You could tell he was just out of police school, but we got past without any problems. The third roadblock was better; the police were more amiable, and we got through easily.

About thirty kilometers before the Brazilian border, we stopped at a house, which we had anticipated might be necessary. It was a safe place with friends who put us up as long as necessary, so we could leave when things had cooled off. We had foreseen that the border was going to be very difficult. Ramón couldn't risk being identified, and we knew that Argentine security was helping the Paraguayans in the manhunt. The thing that worried me the most was that they might publish photos of Ramón, which would make it very difficult for us to leave legally. Ramón had already prepared for a clandestine exit via the river if that became necessary. That was the alternate plan.

The border was closed for a good many days, and that created lots of problems. That delirious madman, Stroessner, closed up the country as if he were slamming his front door shut. We knew what was happening along the border. There were lots of people with children who had no place to stay, nothing to eat. They were sleeping in their cars, without blankets, and it was raining. It was general chaos.

Ana continued her story:
I kept listening to the radio all night, and Thursday morning I bought the newspaper which said that the border was closed. The paper carried the names of Santiago and of a woman they confused with Julia. I called travel agencies to see if the Asunción airport was also closed. They told me yes, but about 11:00 a.m. they said that the airport had been opened for incoming planes, so I went to the airport. I had a ticket, but no reservation, so I placed myself on the waiting list. Since lots of people were canceling their reservations for Paraguay, I was able to get a seat.

I arrived in Asunción on Thursday, the 18th at 3:00 p.m. Everything seemed normal, and they didn't even check my baggage. I took a taxi to the hotel that Ramón had indicated. I had arranged the first meeting with Santiago for 4:00 p.m. in a zone that swarmed with people, not far from Santiago's safe house. I did my best to arrive on time, but I couldn't get there until 4:15. He wasn't there. I thought that surely, because the papers had published his Identi-Kit portrait, that he was waiting for our 6:00 p.m. meeting when it would be getting dark. At 6:00 I went to the alternate site, which was a street corner near the first place. I got there early and waited nearly an hour, making myself visible and searching each face. I drew near each passerby to make sure it wasn't Santiago. He didn't show up.

There was no problem with the location of the meeting. It was a place he could get to even if he had to sneak through the underbrush, and there were few passersby.

I returned to the hotel and started watching television.

I didn't understand anything. The situation was getting worse by the minute. First, we had the bad luck that within ten hours of the operation they had already identified Santiago. The next day, his photo came out. I knew he was in danger. Despite all the plans we had made, it never occurred to us that he would be so badly burnt by the next day. Our situation when we got together would be very difficult. If he hadn't shown up at either meeting, it was because he had a serious problem. He was wearing a beard, and in the photo he appeared with only a mustache. Besides, it wasn't a photo; it was an Identi-Kit construction. I was hoping that he might not be too recognizable. I waited impatiently for Friday when the two appointments would be repeated.

I stayed in my room watching television and listening to the radio. There were several television and mobile radio units broadcasting. One was from the Somoza residence. They said Somoza's son had arrived. The radio broadcast false reports. They said they had found the woman who accompanied Santiago, that there had been a shooting in such and such a place.

At 10:00 p.m. a mobile unit went to Santiago's safe house. They said there had been a lengthy shootout. I didn't want to believe it, but they gave the story, step by step. The operation lasted several hours, and there were still police in the house. First reports said it was a confrontation with some thieves. Later, they said there was a death, and apparently it was Santiago. An hour went by, and they announced that the police had invited the press to police headquarters to view the body and identify it. They described Santiago and the way he was dressed. After that, they filmed the interior of the house, filmed the sofa where the arms had been hidden, the Uruguayan passport, the $4,000, and the stamps with which I was going to fix Santiago's passport.

The Paraguayan police had two starting points in their investigation into the death of Somoza: the operational house where the action was carried out, and the Chevrolet pickup that was abandoned fifty meters from the scene with the weapons inside it. The following is an attempt to reconstruct their procedure:

While one team interviewed the owner of the house and the watchman, obtaining a physical description of Julia and the details of the Julio Iglesias cover story, another team checked used car lots until they encountered the person who had sold the pickup to Osvaldo. This man associated Santiago, a tall, bearded redhead, with Osvaldo, whose features he had nearly forgotten. The watchman at the operational house also described Ramón. The common denominator that linked the four was the fact that, from their appearance as well as their accents, they were obviously Argentines. The Argentine security police were alerted from the beginning to help crack the case. They took it for granted that the commando team was made up of experienced members of the Montoneros or the ERP, and as soon as the Identi-Kits had been prepared, they identified Santiago by his true name, Hugo Irurzún. There was also a fairly accurate Identi-Kit image of Julia, but the Argentine police mistakenly identified her as Silvia Mercedes Hodgens, a former militant of the ERP, who at that time was living in Mexico.

The Identi-Kit likenesses were published in the morning papers on Thursday, September 18, and President Stroessner offered a reward of 4 million *guaranís* to anyone who could provide information as to the whereabouts of members of the commando team. At this point, the couple who had rented a room to Santiago and Ana during their first week in Asunción came forward, identifying Santiago and providing a description of Ana. With these leads, the police undoubtedly verified the approximate date when the couple rented their safe house and checked with the various real estate agencies in Asunción to learn what houses had been rented during that period. Another possibility was that the local storekeeper recognized Santiago from the Identi-Kit portrait and gave police the location of his safe house. The indisputable fact was that the police worked rapidly and efficiently.

Julia tells of her feelings of insecurity after her Identi-Kit was published in the papers:

In Argentina we felt supported by the people. We knew that

nobody, except a policeman, would denounce us. In the final instance, they might not help us, but they wouldn't do anything against us. My problem was that in Paraguay we had to endure the tension of knowing that there were five million policemen on our trail. I felt that people were staring at me, that men were following me with their eyes.

Ramón told us:
We don't know why Santiago was in the house when the police arrived. According to our arrangements, he shouldn't have been there. We suppose he must have had some difficulty in entering the house. Perhaps there was some sort of police activity in the area, and he put off his return until the following day to pick up the things he needed from there.

After dropping off Osvaldo, he was supposed to go directly to the safe house, shave off his beard and go to another hideout close to the site of his meeting with Ana. But when the photograph of his cadaver appeared in the newspapers, he was still wearing a full beard. Undoubtedly there was some difficulty that kept him from entering the house. He had to wait, and when he finally was about to enter or was already inside, the police arrived.

The news of Santiago's death profoundly moved all the members of the team. Armando and Susana, Ramón and Julia, all had to hide their grief from the people who had given them shelter, but at least they could console each other when they were alone. Ana's case was different. She had no one with whom she could talk, and with each passing day her danger increased, because she had been identified as Santiago's companion:

There were some people who were suspicious of me because I was alone, because they saw something in my face. There were people who asked me, "Have you been crying?"

However hard I tried to act like a tourist, some people noticed my sorrow.

Santiago's parents arrived the following day. His mother was suffering and didn't want to speak, but his father agreed to talk to reporters. He said he wanted to identify his son,

that he hadn't been able to find the official who would turn
the corpse over to him, that he was going through the
bureaucratic procedures to recover the body, but they didn't
want to turn it over. Finally, their limited entry visa expired
and they had to return without their son's body.

Santiago's father was a very rigid person, and they'd had
differences over Santiago's political militancy, but now he
made a lovely declaration. He said he felt terribly proud of
his son, and he told how much he respected and loved him
and how intelligent and good he had been. He raised up
Santiago and he totally vindicated his memory. Santiago
always had a close relationship with his mother, but not with
his father, and I know he always wanted to hear such a
response from his father.

Ana's Uruguayan passport had the same entry stamp as that
on Santiago's, which the police had confiscated.

I couldn't leave the country on that passport, Ana told us,
and I had to wait until the situation had quieted down a bit.
I wasn't worried that I would be recognized because I wasn't
known in the safe house neighborhood, and besides, I had
changed my appearance, dyed my hair and everything. The
hotel people knew I had arrived the day after the operation,
and I took pains to establish warm relations with them, to
not appear suspicious. I invented a whole story: that I had
come for a short stay and afterwards I would return to Brazil
to rejoin my family, but while the border was closed I was
unable to leave.

After about six days, the authorities issued an edict that
all foreigners who wanted to leave the country had to present
themselves at the Office of Investigations and obtain a pink
card that would permit them to circulate freely. I was caught
in a gridlock. I couldn't stay in my hotel room day and night;
I had to act like a tourist.

A week after my arrival I caught a bus to go out and
take some photos of an Indian reservation. There was a
roadblock even before we left Asunción and we were asked
to show our documents. I had to get down from the bus, and

I started arguing. They told me it was a rapid procedure and it was necessary in order to circulate freely, because there was a detention order out for all foreigners. They made me wait there together with a boy and two girls who were Uruguayan and Argentine respectively. We were waiting for a police car to come and take us to the police station. The truth is, I could have escaped during that interim, but I thought it was better to try bluffing my way through. On the way to the police station, I hid $200 I was carrying between the seat cushions, because those bills were of the same series as the $4,000 the police had found in the safe house.

In the police station, the man who took our statements was half-asleep. I tried to evaluate everything. Here again, I could have run out the door because he wasn't armed. But what was I to do without the circulation permit? I was optimistic, because I saw they weren't pressuring us; it was simply a general roundup. To try to escape would only have complicated my situation, and I wanted to postpone any complications as long as possible.

They had our documents, and they herded us in to take our statements. All of this created enormous disorder because of the number of new transactions involved.

First, they called the Uruguayan to make his statement, and they let him go. Another plain-clothes policeman came in and asked, "How many are there?"

"Only three. Take them away."

We walked two blocks to the Office of Investigations, with this unarmed plain-clothes man ahead and us trailing along behind him. A total absurdity. They made us wait in another hall which was even more chaotic than the first. On the second floor there were lots of men crowded into a large cell, and on the floor below in an open room there were a whole bunch of women milling around, going to the toilet, crying. These people had been picked up on the streets, in different neighborhoods, in general police dragnets because they had no identification. I sat down to wait there, asking myself what was going to happen to me.

Susana recalls:

After a few days we drove to Encarnación and learned they were detaining all foreigners. We returned to our friends' place, and they said, "Stay here. Don't go back to Encarnación or they'll put you in jail."

There we remained. We let more time go by, and one day Armando went back with the farmer to Encarnación. They walked in like two peasants, leaving the car on the outskirts, and Armando saw that the situation had changed. We loaded the suitcases into the car, drove to Encarnación and left them abandoned along with the car. Armando bought some auto repair parts, and I bought some knitting wool. Auto parts are hard to get in Argentina, and wool is cheaper in Paraguay. We left everything else behind and entered Argentina with the clothes on our backs and with the money and our passports hidden.

Armando told us:
When Susana and I crossed the border, we didn't go through any bureaucratic routines. We didn't get an exit permit or anything. When we got to the Argentine side, we walked off the boat normally, and they told us, "No, to enter the country you need an exit permit from Paraguay."

We had to return to Paraguay, and I befriended the man in charge there. I told him, "Look, I have this problem. I crossed over this morning to buy these parts, and I didn't go through the formal procedures. Now, with the way things are these days, they're asking me for papers."

"I know," he said. "Just wait here."

They kept us there for an hour, gave me the papers, and we caught the next launch to Argentina.

Susana continues:
When we got to Posadas, we took a bus immediately and got out of there, Once inside Argentina, we had the problem of our past history. We traveled all day long. At night we got off at a certain city, registered at a hotel, and because of the state of our nerves, we spent the night drinking whatever we could get our hands on: soft drinks, wine, hard liquor. We didn't get any sleep, but neither did we get drunk. We were talking,

talking, talking, making plans to get out of the country as quickly as possible. The problem was that we had to buy clothing, plane tickets, all of those things. We did that the following morning and caught a plane for Río. Since Brazil is a neighboring country, we didn't need a visa.

Julia wore her hair long in Paraguay, but when she went to rent the operational house, she took the precaution of gathering it up. She told us:

Neither the watchman nor the owner of the house ever saw me with my hair down, but the hotel porter did. I was careful, and I used dark glasses and all that, but there was a burnt-out bulb in my room, and there are times when one lets down one's guard. I called the desk, and when the porter came in to repair the light, he saw me with my hair loose, without dark glasses, and without makeup. My Identi-Kit was exactly like that.

When I saw that photo, I immediately cut my hair, of course. That turned out to be a tremendous error, because next day all the papers printed the photo of the *compañera* in Mexico, who really looks a lot like me, and her photo showed her with hair exactly as short as mine. What saved me when I crossed the border was the fact that I was pregnant.

Despite the fact that I was the most badly burnt publicly and the one everybody was looking for, I had to be the one to cross the border first, because we didn't know whether or not Ramón had been identified. When I saw the Immigration inspector, I told myself, "If I get across safely, I'm not going to believe it."

I told the man I was pregnant and very upset, and it was incredible that my husband had to stay on the Brazilian side, and look at these medical certificates that prove I'm having problems with my pregnancy. And meanwhile I was looking at everybody and searching the walls to see if they had a "Wanted" photo of Ramón, so I could warn him as soon as I got through. My Identi-Kit photo was there, and Santiago's, but I didn't see any others. A man behind a sort of teller's window had my photo, and I started talking and talking to distract them, and it worked. I didn't want to cross over by myself, because it was night and I was afraid something might happen, and couldn't one of them accompany me?

I talked so much that they threw up their hands and said, "Go on through, lady."

Ramón told us:
We had information that the border was back to normal, and we chose the day of the week and the hour we thought would be best. We planned everything carefully. Julia crossed over first, saw that everything was in order, and she let me know. The following day I went through, complying with all the legal Immigration and Customs requirements. As a precaution, I disguised myself carefully, because I was worried that the Argentine security police had distributed photos of all possible participants, starting with the best-known, most-wanted individuals.

Once I got across the border I rejoined Julia and we left for Spain to join the rest of the group there.

Susana continues the story of their getaway:
We arrived in Río at night. I had been in that airport many times. I knew all the combinations and where to buy tickets, and I told Armando, "I'm going to resolve all this right now so that, if we can't leave immediately for Europe, we'll be on the first plane tomorrow." I got tickets for a flight that left at 6:00 a.m. Because we were leaving so early, we had priority for a room in the airport hotel. It was the first night I really slept well, even if it was only for four or five hours.

The following morning while she was waiting in the airport for their plane to leave, Susana saw Osvaldo smiling at her mockingly from in front of the magazine-stand. Their encounter was completely accidental. Susana nudged Armando.

"Look at our news-stand boy," she said, and Armando got up and followed his friend into the men's room, which was filled with other passengers. They occupied adjoining urinals but didn't say a word to each other. Before leaving, Osvaldo raised a hand discreetly and formed a circle with his thumb and forefinger to indicate that everything was going smoothly. On the plane for Europe, he sat four rows ahead of Susana and Armando, but they all waited until they arrived at Madrid airport before engaging in conversation.

Ana continues the account of her odyssey:

I tried to talk to about twenty policemen in Investigations, and they took the resigned attitude that all this was a meaningless formality, because none of these people had had anything to do with the Somoza operation. After a few hours they let me join the other women in the main hall, who told me they had had their fingerprints taken. After about an hour they called me into the office of the political police where they took my statement, asked me what I was doing in Paraguay, what day I had entered, where I was staying and if I had any criminal record: all of this as if they were begging my pardon. And they didn't bother to take my fingerprints.

All in all, I spent two days and two nights without sleep, waiting for them to come and get me. I was ready for them to take me away for interrogation at any moment, but despite this I was calm. I was happy that we had carried out our mission successfully. I had heard about the Nicaraguans declaring a day of National Jubilation, and I thought, what a party that must have been. Nothing that might happen after that was of any importance to me.

We slept on the floor with newspapers under us. They fed us. Nobody mentioned the operation, and I didn't either. The comments were all about how they had been roused out of bed, taken out of their houses, what things had happened to them. In the midst of all this, I spoke to a policeman whom one of the girls told me was the softest of all of them, and I asked him to phone my hotel so they would know I was detained and they would save my room and my things. I told him once again that I hadn't entered Paraguay until the day after Somoza was killed. This was my strongest argument. The policeman went personally to speak to the hotel manager and brought me a reply, saying, "Don't worry, they're keeping everything for you at the hotel. I asked the chief to look into your case, and you'll be able to leave soon."

That left me more at ease. I imagine they checked the Interpol Wanted list and then made sure I really had entered the country on September 18. On Saturday, they read off a list of people who were to be released, and my name was on it. We had to stand in line to recover our passports. Mine apparently had been there all the time, because it was in the same drawer where they had placed it when I was picked up, and we all had to help the policeman sort out which was which.

They gave me my passport on Saturday at 2 p.m., and they finally took my fingerprints for the circulation permit that allowed me to leave the country.

I had hidden the rest of my money in the hotel room. I packed my bag, and on Saturday afternoon I caught the bus for Presidente Stroessner, passing through seven or eight army roadblocks by showing my passport and the card proving I had been identified. I got through without any problems. At the border I caught a taxi and at the Customs shed I showed my passport and pink card from inside the cab. They let me through without stamping anything. That's how I entered Brazil and from there continued traveling to join my *compañeros*.

Ana was the last one out, Susana told us. It wasn't until she arrived that I was able to release all the bottled-up tension. We were desperate because it took her so long, and we clung to each other and wept. That was what finally relaxed me.

EPILOGUE

The night before our last interview with Armando and Ana, we watched a television film made by an American group on the lookout for strong emotions. They were aboard a whaling ship that had a cage of steel bars slung alongside the hull. A camera crew filmed sharks slicing off chunks of whale blubber from the carcasses alongside the ship. At a certain point, members of the team opened the door of the cage and swam out to film the blood-crazed sharks at the peak of their feeding frenzy, with only an electric cattle prod to protect them. This spectacle and the book we were writing brought to mind *Manhunt*, a novel written by Geoffrey Household shortly after World War II. In the novel, a British big-game hunter tracks Adolf Hitler down in his eagle's nest at Berchtesgaden, has him in the telescopic sights of his rifle and, inexplicably, refuses to pull the trigger.

The next day, after the interviews, we asked the two of them:

"Wasn't there some element of challenge, a sense of going after the most dangerous game in the world, that added a special emotional charge to your project?"

Ana replied:

Not on my part. It was a political operation, and a matter of political conviction. The worst thing that could have happened to Somoza had already happened, and that was to have been dethroned. It seemed to me important that he should pay for the terrible crimes he had committed. We felt the project was inspiring, a way of serving justice for all the violent deaths and all the injustices that are committed each day in Latin America.

Besides that, not a single one of us ever wanted to be

identified. The only way Ramón's identity became known was because of a violation of confidence on the part of a news-paperman. This is a measure of the fact that nobody wanted to boast about our participation in the operation. The more anonymous we remained, the better, not only for reasons of personal security but because none of us had any interest in achieving notoriety.

Armando puffed out his cheeks and exhaled heavily when we posed the question, and as he listened to Ana's reply he clenched his fists with barely-contained emotion.

I don't resent the question or anything like that, and I understand why you asked it. I've seen lots of these television programs in which people jump out of planes and don't open their parachutes until the last moment, in search of personal thrills. This happens in societies where there are limited horizons. The individual in that kind of society, where values are twisted, seeks strong emotions to exalt his own existence.

It isn't accidental that this sort of thrill-seeking doesn't exist in Latin America. I've never heard of anyone throwing himself out of a plane or anything like that. Life, for us, is very difficult. Simply to be born a working stiff or an ordinary person in Latin America is enough of an adventure. One has to struggle in order to eat, in order to stay alive from day to day. This is what motivates us. In every military operation, we experience fear, lots of fear. What happens is that, with practical experience and with the strength of our convictions, we manage to overcome this fear.

We would be much happier if imperialism didn't exist, if exploitation didn't exist. For us, this isn't thrill-seeking; it's a deep conviction that we have to do something about the situation; it is a social necessity. We would be much happier if we could lead normal, tranquil lives. Just as one example, I haven't seen my children for the past five years. For me, this isn't a sport; it's a real sacrifice. We are convinced that as long as the imperialists are determined to exploit our people, and as long as small minorities flourish at the expense of hunger, suffering, and the deaths of hundreds of thousands of children, we have to do something; we have to fight back. We have to resolve a historical problem. We are no different than many other people who are involved in a life and death struggle.

I left Paraguay with a bleeding ulcer. It took me three months to get it under control. That isn't a romantic experience. We don't really enjoy living out this type of emotion. The fact is that we are convinced that we have to do these things to put an end to a rotten system. We cannot tolerate the existence of millionaire playboys while thousands of Latin Americans are dying of hunger. We are perfectly willing to give up our lives for this cause. We are willing to do all of this conscientiously, but not because we like it. We don't like to kill; if we do it, it is to put an end to the killing.

You can talk about people who die in military confrontations; talk about people who die in battle; but what about children who die of hunger and disease? Aren't they just as dead? We have to put an end to all...of this. Put an end to torture, put an end to hunger. This is why we do what we do, not because we like it, I repeat, nor because we are heroes in a suspense novel, nor super-agents who nourish themselves on danger.

All of that is false. We are terribly frightened, but the conviction that we have to do these things is greater than the fear we may feel. One thing is true: at the moment when one acts, one forgets everything. Once the action is over, our legs start trem-bling. That's a psychological problem.

When they were torturing me in Argentina, the torturers commented to each other, "This sonofabitch won't talk," they said, "because he's a yogi, because he's been brainwashed, because he's been super-trained."

That is the kind of explanation they give each other, because they don't think the way we do, because they don't know what it is to have a strong conviction. They think it's something super-natural. They can't understand why we refuse to talk.

I think it's very important that you say this: we who executed Somoza are not highly-trained super agents; that our motive was not to live in luxury hotels, sleep with ten different women, travel around in airplanes. No. We are *compañeros* who experience fear and whose fearlessness does not lie in thrill-seeking nor in taking risks in order, as those people would say, to relish the flavor of life.

For us, the flavor of life is that there will be no more hunger, no exploitation, no misery. That is the flavor of life. We aren't adventurers. We are revolutionaries with all the fears, the doubts, the failings, the problems, that everyone else has. We quarrel amongst ourselves, and in the moment of action, our legs tremble. Not in the moment of action, but ten minutes later, our legs tremble.

CURBSTONE PRESS, INC.

is a non-profit publishing house dedicated to literature that reflects a
commitment to social change, with an emphasis on contemporary writing
from Latino, Latin American and Vietnamese cultures. Curbstone presents
writers who give voice to the unheard in a language that goes beyond
denunciation to celebrate, honor and teach. Curbstone builds bridges
between its writers and the public – from inner-city to rural areas, colleges to
community centers, children to adults. Curbstone seeks out the highest
aesthetic expression of the dedication to human rights and intercultural
understanding: poetry, testimonies, novels, stories,
and children's books.

This mission requires more than just producing books. It requires ensuring
that as many people as possible learn about these books and read them. To
achieve this, a large portion of Curbstone's schedule is dedicated to
arranging tours and programs for its authors, working with public school
and university teachers to enrich curricula, reaching out to underserved
audiences by donating books and conducting readings and community
programs, and promoting discussion in the media. It is only through these
combined efforts that literature can truly make a difference.

Curbstone Press, like all non-profit presses, depends on the support of
individuals, foundations, and government agencies to bring you, the reader,
works of literary merit and social significance which might not find a place
in profit-driven publishing channels, and to bring the authors and their
books into communities across the country. Our sincere thanks to the many
individuals, foundations, and government agencies who have recently
supported this endeavor: Community Foundation of Northeast Connecticut,
Connecticut Commission on Culture & Tourism, Connecticut Humanities
Council, Fertel Foundation, Greater Hartford Arts Council, Hartford
Courant Foundation, Lannan Foundation, National Endowment for the
Arts, and the United Way of the Capital Area.

Please help to support Curbstone's efforts to present the diverse voices and
views that make our culture richer. Tax-deductible donations can be made
by check or credit card to:
Curbstone Press, 321 Jackson Street, Willimantic, CT 06226
phone: (860) 423-5110 fax: (860) 423-9242
www.curbstone.org

my sweet unconditional

ariel robello

Tia Chucha Press
Los Angeles

ACKNOWLEDGMENTS
With all honor and respect to the Creator/a whose guidance has made the journey possible.
I ask your help for the road ahead.
With mil gracias to my mother for never giving up on me.
With love for my father who taught me to look at the world with a painter's eye.
With a song for my family on the other side, in my heart there are no lines between us.
With humble affection for the writing communities of The World Stage, PEN West, Los Angeles, San
Diego, San Francisco, New York and Washington DC—you have all inspired me to step out of my shell
and brave the work everyday.
With props to my students for their support, your poems are the glue in my life.
With much respect for Luis and Tia Chucha Press for keeping your word and seeing that my words found
their way to these pages, I look forward to the work ahead.
With love to my friends whose enduring belief and unconditional love allowed me to see the
dream through.

ISBN 1-882688-29-5

Book design: Jane Brunette
Cover illustration: Serina Koester, Ariel Robello and Rhea Vedro
Back cover photo: Justin M. Jobst

PUBLISHED BY: DISTRIBUTED BY:
Tía Chucha Press   Northwestern University Press
PO Box 328   Chicago Distribution Center
San Fernando CA 91341   11030 South Langley Avenue
                                       Chicago IL 60628

Tía Chucha Press is supported by the National Endowment for the Arts and operating funds from Tía Chucha's
Centro Cultural – www.tiachucha.com.

TABLE OF CONTENTS

LA GATA

1

I drank to drown my pain,
but the damned pain learned how to swim,
and now I'm overwhelmed
by this decent and good behavior.

FRIDA KAHLO

ANGELES ASADA

They are burning the bodies tonight.

The crematorium on 8th Street don't hide its stench
from the staggered silhouettes of drunken men
who spend every cent on brown-bagged bottles of hope
tonight the barrio hums *De Colores* and low rider tunes
as people cope with fragrant asada of human flesh
shielded in hibiscus pink and Acapulco blue homes
these nights a test for spirits stuck in crude oil of fronteralands.

Memo squashes black ants with his bare feet
under an orange moon I trace my name in the stars
we own this hillside view
where ghettos are fallen galaxies
and poverty she is down right pretty tonight.

You promised we would live free... "mas alla de la razon"
and that "all would be alright"
only here, there is no magic carpet ride
no up and away
just Memo blowing *El Rey* on a blade of dry grass
and a German shepherd's ears tuned to renegade radio station.

Tune out Miranda   tune in revolution   baby

Memo whispers wet Spanglish in my ear
but all I hear is the woman next door praying between sobs
hoping God will subdue her old man's temper
Memo can't hear what wars he's survived
her screams like shrapnel won't penetrate his thick skin
his hand weaves its way between my thighs
and Mr. DJ say *all is all right*   *yeah*   *all is all right*
only here, there is no magic carpet ride
no up and away
just a tagging crew playing quarters
on the unmarked tomb of a forgotten soldier.

Hungry for coconut juice and cool ripe melon
we slow dance into K-LOVE late night forgiveness
then make love on an old mattress
Memo strung out on sky, me strung out on fear
cause that's how we collect strikes
at the intersection where first generation and ancient meet
where corn vendors and chrome saddle cement
where shopping carts and homeboys come home bent
and every one counts angels making their way through the sky.

Cause here, there is no magic carpet ride
no up and away for the living
no shiny pennies
early refunds
or middle age
from smoke stack to lung
hope steams crooked, sweet tipped and tender
as the bodies burn I let myself surrender
to the only thing that never changes
my love for the boy who plays Mariachi on the wings of daisies.

SUS CONSEJOS

Mama said, "Latin loves don't last long."
(stick to your own kind)
she knows how hard
to sleep so good
too late for her
for me he's gone
under my skin another splinter
under my sheet another crumb.

Papa said, "You want a doctor, someone to take care of you."
(stick to your own kind)
he knows how hard to slap
brown on white won't stick
he knew he'd quit
he knew love lies
in my bed
under my skin
sticking not stuck.

"Stick to your own kind, m'ija."
I know to last
I must deny love of self
to find my kind
I know they said they know what's best
but still I make my love in mud.

HOME

where I'm from real people eat tacos at 4 a.m.
drunk and high they enjoy freedom of D

                                       R

                                           O

                                             P top

low
low
low riders
with neon bass and no where
no where to go
real people lie steal and smoke their lives away
angry and undereducated
real people need drama and day jobs
to occupy voids between hangovers
and month late car payments

confined to waiting rooms
real people stare down
real people under florescent lights
they print their names at the X with a lucky pen
for a chance at free checking and chest exams

with security cameras watching
real people dance with mannequins
after closing real people sweat
under heat lamps their bodies melding
into one seamless happy ending

once a flaming rabbit's foot
fell through the black top
of my real world
the roof
the roof
the roof is on fire
it was the first time

i.   la gata loca
saw a hole to the other side
where the best years of real life
were worth more than a slow dance with number 33
on the all star team

for me the thunder of my feet
pounding what's real into molehills behind me
is as loud as the night I decided to hunt the wildebeest of more

LET ME RIDE

let me ride in the lover's car
where I am Iztaccihuatl on his lap
white volcano before war
bass rumbling below us
warnings from fault lines undecided
which side we'll choose

it takes an hour to go one mile down the Strip
that is three lights
his fingers tapping Morse code inside
the lover's car where bras are left like surrender flags
and perfect bald heads grow wet with cinnamon kisses

I want to be the Aztec calendar girl
mounted between his shrine to la Virgin and Teena Marie
hickeys framing my charm necklace
laughing at bullhorn warnings
from policemen too afraid to talk shit to our faces

it is before curfew, graduation and Uncle Sam's nagging plea
to be all you can be on this night
you must ride, 15 mph, detailed and louder than your neighbor
you must know which hand signs peace and which will launch wanton action
you must bite down hard on your urge to outrun
every other hard shell in the race

let me ride backseat immune to stop signs
pilfering seconds before life calls
before we become hazy interpretations of what they'd have us be
before laptops and DSL, Afghanistan and dress pants
before credit checks, regrets, training camps, freshman politics, rudimentary
skills we'll need to survive after this night
steady driver, we're making time stand still back here
steady, we're undressing worm holes back here
steady, we ain't ready to go home just yet

TUFF MEDICINE

Oye nena!
this poem is tuff medicine
made up of 2 parts naked storm
3 part mercenary men
4 part petalpusher
1 part oxygen

I dub dub dare ya
become electric buttafly
come on sour angel stop frontin
you holdin up traffic in your veins
you slumlordin your soul

precious peahen penned into your "Stories"
dying to dig up roots of someone else's pain
no one won here
worse yet
no one ever will

dig this vision
one twelve foot neon WIC sign
it took six men to climb the pole
black birds with fat bellies
to align the holes
just right   all day   all night
you keep your Venus intact
cry anti-freeze
when he's late to your 3 a.m. dream
the one when you ride Coney Island's *Earthquake*
10 times in a row
shaken from outside-in
you find a way to forgive

from top twin tenement towers
Big Boi screams   *Perdoname!*
into a universal megaphone
they come quick
take him in for inciting a riot

it takes life to live here
steady hands to hold the rails

child I dub dub dare ya
play the panic down
calm your tracks with cocoa butta
and become sweet face of nowhere

THE NIGHT THE DJ SAVED MY LIFE

for New York after hours

his eyes split the dance floor

his lips split the groove of my smile
his vinyl smooth caress took one breast and fed an island nation
between the ebb and his tongue
a spinning table of reasons
why not
come
undone

we stood erect
pulsing time into timba
laughter then dip into back board marimba
equal shots of mambo & lime
his finger epidermal needles
retracting inhibition from my spine
in   slow   slide   scratch
we held our breath exhaled and came in time

sigh   all that's left of the DJ that saved my life
is a mixed tape and over 18 glowing under black light

RAVE POLITICS

you can look but don't touch the butterflies
an angel is a death trap with wings
space aliens are open to solicitations
white pills will make your skin peel off
the blue ones will put it back on
don't take a first date
if your friends multiply before your eyes
take off the glasses
if they grow another head
gently push it back in
a bad dancer is probably a Narc
not everybabydoe is looking at you
two is boring
three or more is showbiz
when you take off in the red balloon don't look down
when you land   don't look up
fire-breathing dragons will deflate
when driving into nowhere gas up and buy tic tacs
to   t   r   a   i   l   behind you
if glass shards spin all around
pretend they're sugar plum fairies
but whatever you do never
no never stop dancing

RAPPER'S DELIGHT

hello of cleavage
cinch of stretch denim
poison sprayed cross your ass & chest

against the wall you a Malaysian carving
invisible basket of dreams balanced on your head
your curves calling men to reel you in

the back seat a sweat lodge
frost of nights you called home from pay phone
half whimper half spit
left because you wouldn't —
no couldn't — why do you resist?

and how they scorned your rebellion
threw the mic in your face
back stage a race to the after party
where they took turns inside you
while you'd wait for your Savior to come

in hotel lobby they'd rub reason and meter
in your ears a buzz of something you had to say
burning behind your teeth a wad of gum
clicking tongue of paces

you blew on the dice
won a shadow deal behind emcee of the week
graduate of street games (invented and real)
emory board routine on acrylic nails
filing holes in your head heart womb
where poem or love or baby might have grown
had you'd owned your free will

against the wall you look angelic
wide-eyed with magnetic pull of spotlights
high of his hand moving up your thigh

see girl, a rapper's delight always delivers sunshine
until she's sent home at sunrise black-eyed and broken

THE RUNWAY

Hailey's comet tears down La Cienega Blvd.
splitting the car wash
open like a hooker's thighs

blisters rise on Randy's giant doughnut
sweet confections and garbage men
scramble for their lives

the unfortunate driver
stuck at the eternal red light
glass cut palms
a lifetime of gripping the wheel
too tight

the misunderstood sky
a field of bloody salutations
waving hello

goodbye.

IN YOUR FACE LOVE

trapped in cul-de-sacs and Denny's bathrooms
the loyal are tested to see how much split your bottom lip can take
on the other side of love is a brown boy
who never meant to hurt you

asleep in alleys and on stained sheets at Motel 6
the one between Pal's Happy Liquor and Emerald City Express
with noodles and malt beer to fill the dying beast
in your face love forgets which hand struck first
who did what when and why even friends don't question no more

spider web in the corner
prey tired and sufficiently numb
the hourglass on your neck
accessory to a crime you'll claim you like it rough
each welt proof enough
you're no body 'til somebody loves you

in your face love like the first 18 days in Vietnam
a lifetime of seizures
virgin nostrils in a field of rusty poppies
like winter in Belgrade and summer in Harlem
in your face love's a lightening rod in the grip of an iron man
a covenant of Sunday slow jams
a Rolls Royce in quick sand
in your face love is La Motta vs. Sugar Ray 1951
in the 13th round saying I never went down
no, for this love I stood standing

CARTA PERSONAL

Abuelita's hands wake me
soft as masa they tell of maquiladora murders
young girls left crumpled, braids cut off
bits of pay slips found under pink nails
they warn of an invisible plague that has invaded my mother
red armies taking over honest cells.

Glaring pixels blind eyes too tired to sleep
as the dial up begins my fingers lament the deserts between us
under each key a child's skull from the graves of Monzote
under each rock the echo of two 4th graders at war
their scissors still chasing each other around Room 11
with a hate as open and hungry as the Grand Canyon.

My sweet unconditional,
what of the woman who changed her name to Lola
boarded a Greyhound and crossed state-after-state to see
if she'd make the same mistakes as far from him as she could get
and what of lovers hunted by mosquitoes in Managua
their dark flesh hidden by banana leaves
depressed breezes flirting with their nipples
will the scars of their scratching show come dawn?

What of the screams of the mute
do they leave from the eyes
and do those same eyes extract memory from tears
enough to start a new blue planet
those piercing red layers of granite between us
like the painted walls of Palenque
what amount of dynamite would it take to break into a heart that stiff?

My sweet unconditional,
there is no one to send these questions to but you

tonight an anonymous brick went through the window of Mr. Lim's market
landing one shoplifter dead.
My love do curses brand the same in Korean
and if they do where can we market this rage?
There is sadness at 3 a.m. at 4 and at 5
there is dawn then duty
pinned to my mattress
tattooed to last night's neck
spelled in pink crosses along the ravine
our love, an s.o.s. straddled over time.

OVER PASS-T DUE CONFESSION

I.

Under the overpass two boys walked
parading gold-dipped silver chains
breast plate crosses & Nike signs, size of sunspots
enough to catch the eye of our would-be leader

II.

I knew the short one from Kindergarten
where we shared a box
his name on top
and I'd hated him for it

a good girl would have looked away
when the tall one's veins burst
frightened moons covered with webs of red licorice
a good girl would have ran when his kneecaps shattered
sound like lunar rover landing

III.

today there are HBO specials
that could make this suburban horror real for you non-believers
this perennial fuck you at the hand of a practice bat
from have not to have less fools

IV.

"e'ry-body deserves a good beat down once in awhile"
that's what they told me and that's what I sold my God
after all *my man* was most beautiful when he'd hit his mark
and sad girls that want to stay happy learn to laugh shit off

V.

shamed I think of the sons I don't have
the ones I dare teach
wound collars of barbed wire nailed to their necks
an ancient scar size of dime bag
settle between their brow
I think of the Amor-all slide that made it easy
to jump in and get away

VI.

Hell is that they went on living
with grandma's waffles and football
to make the work week sweeter
they went on drinking at 4th St. Dicks
planning their revenge on napkins and place mats
but we were a faceless plague
spreading ourselves too thin

VII.

so I laughed the scales
up and down the white ivory of the poor bastard's teeth
my apologies for having nothing better to do that night
than hold my man's chain
while he worked out his rage on the face of someone else's brother

RICO SUAVE

Rico *Suave* liked to lick muñeca virgins
enough to get them loose
and when they closed their eyes
he would slip
bonitas
queridas
and *suavecitas*
down their skirts
let the bass in his Camero do most of the work
while his hands kept time on drumskin hips
their breast like burial mounds
pressed against his black curls
they'd kiss
taste God
swear faith
flower panties drop to the floor
knees deep in zebra print
Suave, el santo, reclined on his throne
a crushed velvet cushion to lean on
while pushing religion down their throats.

THE PREACHER AT VICTORY OUTREACH
SPEAKS TO SAVE MY HOMEBOY'S SOUL

Sinner beware!!
Submit your sin at the feet of Jesus
polish God's shoes with your retired rag
run boys, run round the snake-charmed congregation
your arms raised and chest cocked like Black Mambo.

Spread the word children
with razor sharp prayers let the world know
the homeboy crusade is coming
high as bonfire flame
aiming for your Saturdays and Mondays
in between days
claiming your families as their own.

Visitors, slouching in the back row
we see you, sloppy with the Devil's lies
we've known you as temptation
but not this time
today you are in *Our* house.

My sons, know you are here to suffer
let me carve out your tattoos
letter by letter
until the warrior has been scarred over
until you are a callous of regret and misguided good intentions.

Get a job good citizen
break the Lord off some pocket change
there is Kool-Aid and donuts in the vestibule for members.
Did you bring your ID?
Have your children memorized their Psalm?
Is your wife alone at home?

Brothers, we'll bail you out of your spiritual prison
we'll mortgage your soul
come, lend me your hand
let the Holy Spirit take hold your tongue
don't fight the work of redemption
there is a Heaven right here on Earth
and Vatos are more than welcome.

YARD SALE MAMACITA

Guest starring la Chismosa

I.

The art of language is a white prom dress sprawled on the floor.

Sequins dug deep into old shag
leave you to house-wife luxuries
telenovelas, microwave home cooking and canned frijoles
when the old man lays down
3.50 an hour times sixty
you smile sweet like fifteen
reassure him with your tone
claro mi corazon es suficiente
sometimes you lie to make ends meet.

Two bags in each hand
ankles swollen like summer tics
you waddle from stop sign to stop sign
a dozen eggs, tortillas, crossword book
no one knows the young girl genius
who won the Pomona Elementary Spelling Bee *five times*
no one knows how you once wore a size six
don't you know everyone is beautiful on prom night.

II.

Aches you are too proud to let go
settle into your back like son #1
you stay buried in a Korean blanket
from a sunken sofa you zone into and out of old photos
framed and nailed to the wall
each an altar to the possibilities that haunt you
hijo querido #2 would have come home
had he never called that recruiter back
y el pendejo still calls after son #3
who sits down to do his matemáticas

cause on day he's gonna build you a bridge to paradise
made from foil, cebolla and an endless mile of sunshine.

III.

You tell Lydia, *nosy mujer*
who lives alone with twenty cats next door
that you are of Spanish descent, *una gitana*
you tell her so well, even you start to believe your own lies
a Flamenco firefly
you twirl around a 1972 vacuum
that long since choked on pennies
change best spent on visiting days too far to bus to
6 a.m. to 5 p.m.
yard sale lady
a.k.a. "mamá" "vieja" "mi mujer"
prom queen figure for sale
synched tight round the mannequin's waist
you wait for someone to be blinded by its flat light
hold your breath when it sells for thirty billetes
to la viejita loca, the one crippled in her feet
and as wide as two tires round her waist
she says she will save it for her granddaughter
la que nunca visita.

Here, where only the wind remembers you
bella... vestida de sueños sequins y juventud
she whispers lavender blessings
that make this day more bearable than most.

SUNDAY MOURNING OVER HUEVOS RANCHEROS

another red summer burns your intestines
as you scoop sunshine with limp tortilla
from my kitchen seat I imagine the tubes that kept you alive
each a garden snake in Adam's Eden

your father stretched over the guitar
his mother left him under a broken street lamp
in Ensenada he'd play til his fingers bled
calling her to come home

at the door twin witnesses claim Jehovah is waiting
for your mother faith's a full book of matches
each votive a hungry totem
in her life there have been two kinds of men...

...those that die and those that haven't yet

I know how tight the Reaper holds you
how he buried your umbilical cord in his backyard
like a voodoo curse your carry lead in your belly
tatted prayer hands mask holes in your back

this Sunday there are fresh haircuts to get
a single file line of remaining friends
pallbearers with number in hand
waiting for the Barber to drop his scythe

VIGIL

On the corner of Figueroa & Citron
a lady sits wrapped in black lace
twenty-four candles at her feet
I should not know the number but I do.

As I pass her my speed drops to a crawl
I've fallen into a grave and she is looking down at me
her long black braid a sure rope.

I pull myself up to stand next to her
death stains my chest
glass slivers dug deep into cheeks that no longer bleed
my hands are limp salamanders
my legs rooted lichen.

Together we stare this angel down
her eyes made up with cotton candy blue
a white cotton dress
silent smile tucked away
that day she was late
her class in urban planning started at 6 p.m.
at 5:25 a mid-sized sedan took an accelerated ride
through her cross street
leaving her a mangled web of pages and skin.

For twenty-four days her mother prayed us into slow motion
her sorrow ruled that corner
her child had cities to build
violins to make sing
now parks grow from her feet
and whole blocks are cluttered landscapes of chalk outlines.

On those Saturday nights when SUVs barrel down the center lane
taking out trash cans and strays
those nights when I drive my sober ass home

wailing like a dove set free from a Jalisco jail
I see the victims of impatience lining the road
and I know it should not move this fast
this passing should catch our breath
if only for the length of a light.

HANDBALL IN LINCOLN HEIGHTS

one hundred fifty-eight roaches between my bare feet and the bathroom
twenty-one cold steps from this heap of dusty orange sheets
this must be where the police will find me
smiling like good time girls do right after they've been caught

twenty-one colds steps between my bare feet and the bathroom
at 2 a.m. Lincoln Heights needs lip gloss
why can't I smile like good time girls do right after
in these hills my cell don't work, I am disconnected

2 a.m. and a girl needs lip gloss
what do lovers in favelas do for kicks
no reception, disconnected 1st world bitch
good time girl to the nth degree

this must be what lovers in favelas do for kicks
swat palmetto bugs in makeshift handball courts
good times under cover of stained sheets, 1st world retreat
legacy of bolder women's feet worn in the tile of his abuela's floor

palmetto bug handball
must be where the last girl gave up
the sight of his abuela swatting then stomping tile floor
beady-eyed monsters retreat to the corner

standing where the last girl gave up
scared to wet myself, the sheets, abuela's tile floor
I did not come here to dance with roaches while my hillside gangster sleeps
beady-eyed monster, his legs up in the air

this must be where I come to my senses
find my shoes, pretty pink tanga, entrails of my dignity
run past abuela and out the front door
but being good time to the nth degree
I curl back into the warm body between me and my great expectations

KILLING IS WHAT HE WAS BORN TO DO

like some are born to paint
or pitch or risk their lives for some worthy cause
look miss, a poem just like you like
about real shit miss,
real like OGs get down for
his enemy's lung an impaled birthday balloon hung on the fence
red lint on white of his cap and kicks
revenge for a life of blank pages.

Being teacher I'd asked for a poem
about a memory they couldn't forget
a first kiss
a first hit from their old man
maybe their first trip to the beach
something real that they could still see
when they closed their eyes at night
like light on your corneas after the switch has been pulled down
the ardent echo of something there before.

It was an epic poem for his trigger finger
crescent moon of right thumb
pink from the squeeze
he'd made so many
their eyes like moths under streetlights
silent nods of homeboys piled in bucket seats
the ride back to the crib
where enchiladas were waiting
taste of ash and blood and beans
mud between this death and the others.

He was born to kill,
like only real thugs can
like only real teachers can comprehend
what it's like to shoot an open ended question into a storm cloud.

THANKSGIVING WITH SIN

Sin, he black eye of domino
father Blood
born on backside of industry
end of freeway 5
where Mac trucks clutter veins like clots

at midnight his mother counts alien ships
from her lawn chair
Keith Sweat serenading the block
where Sin, part devil, part man lives
under halo of urban myth

see Sin, under my skin
his kind of brown like Mississippi mud on my stretch marks
like bits of rust under my nails from swing set sessions
after strip poker and two liters of Old English

Sin, ever thankful
sets me and mamma to steamin at 4 a.m.
collards and yams
not even he will eat
turkey meat stuck in my throat
cause Sin don't date skinny girls
cause his babies sit to my right and left

today Sin both father and son
lazy-eyed martyr of a real G's life after all debts been collected
and when I want to play Bonnie to his Clyde
Sin sits up straight
tells me, *this ain't no life for a good girl*
no kind of life at all
but I know all the words to Mr. Sweat's songs
and how to season greens
how to yell domino with as much fire as ice
bet I know how to make any man happy

Sin, now father and politician
kisses my baby fat
takes me by the hand and smacks my ass on my way out
sayin, *good girl you go on home*
before you catch yourself believing you belong

JAMIE

eyes tied back with black lightening
charcoal rope braided behind her
with pomegranate lips split open, Jamie
could not say no.

While we, the restless, went fishing for richer men
she'd wait by the phone
the calls always came at 7 or 10
Lady, do you accept the collect charges?
yes, she said
yes again and again to the men we'd forgotten
yes to men we'd outgrow before their parole.

There was Juan who liked grape soda and dominoes on Sunday.
Tito who smelled like the cologne aisle in Macy's.
Bobby who never knew when to stop laughing.
Wilson with his tired one line,
"Hey baby, did you hurt yourself fallin from heaven?"
and Sweet Tyrone who could outrun the track team of the school
that asked him to leave when he wouldn't return his history book.

Jamie never said no to their speeches
their poems carved on the wall
their requests for more cigarettes more cash more letters
Jamie stayed home chasing away the high gray waves of solitary
but on some nights the waves won
and when we got home Jamie's lightening had run
down her cheeks a flood of black ink.

Guilty of abandoning our loves for good times
we'd dip our fingers in her stained sink
write of how our love would never end
that we'd wait until the Second Coming
for a second chance to hold them again
we'd promise a letter a night
until the warden had drowned in our pages.

Then the days would unwind like hot rollers
and our lips would cry out for shock red
good times would seep out from the radio and back under our skin
but Jamie she stayed on to carry our tears for us
and when I think of women most loved
by wind by storm by ink

I think of Jamie, eyes tied with black lightening
charcoal rope braided behind
her pomegranate lips on the seals of crisp envelopes
buoys for men lost at sea.

A LOVE POEM FOR A HATE CRIME VICTIM
SPREAD OVER THE MALIBU HILLS

twisted bullets thrown up into a sky too blue to hold heaven

seeds bursting with vermilion of lips yet to be kissed

eyes swollen from poison sprays melted into these mountain ranges

here, wanderers wind like rain down paths made by those who dared
      to swallow *lost* whole

let hunger worm its way through their pot bellied bodies like
      an unpolished hollow tip split into clover

clawing through sands fallen through figurine of God's time

born under mosaic arches of the Alhambra

wounded and healing in Nazi, California

hidden thirteen miles below this sea

thirteen years deep into lifelines they cut

and thirteen months later I'm still watching you bleed

Zapata brava bloodstains on orange buttercups

Your aches loiter on stones cut perfect for resting
      by sunlight and patience

can't you see your pain is nesting itself into my poetry

a lone summit on why free trade isn't really free

a hungry pipe bomb left where our unborn baby sleeps

a sickle cell on the back of a dead man's pillow

spreading still through the echo of air force jets

the hum of ancient regrets   over   bound   towards
        a mountain we too faded to climb

love enters swaying lazy like peacebreakbeat on ranchera time

slicing still through streets with names that sound plain dumb in
        Webster framed English

oh baby you do this   with your wind   your easy way

you do this and I know   if I leave   it won't be today.

BURNT
BRIDGES

Behold, how great a matter a little fire kindled.
And the tongue is a fire,
a world of iniquity:
so is the tongue among our members.

JAMES III V.5-6

BATTLE

It has been eight months
since I've looked into the toilet bowl
and seen my reflection spitting up all that is good in me
piercing my thorax with bitten nubs
blunted by years of acid reflux
index and middle worked so consistently
they now host incomplete ovals
where my identity seeped out one meal at a time.

In my locker I kept the books
no one thought it would occur to me to read.
In my house I kept score of who was winning the war,
my mother or me.
You'd think she would've noticed the cover up
water running, leftovers left on the plate
but she was busy reclaiming her body
putting on pounds he had denied her for years
it was fear that kept her bird boned and emptied.

In Psych 101 they say it is a white girl's disease
brought on by years of exposure to Vogue
sour lilies on a waif mother's vanity
a tea party of sunken skeletons
working their way through skin with gossip and tweezers
and maybe it was the white girl in me wishing her way to the front
through the layers of hip and sway
to the front where college recruiters could see her
all blonde and lean and shake her hand
without fear of contamination.

And maybe it is the white girl who is lonely now
that there are no ulcers guarding her burden
lost she wanders the mountain ranges of my body
wondering when I let go

but I know better
this battle is old habit
one like any other racist twitch
and it lives in the repetition of unloving everything we are
starving all cells equally until you become something other than yourself.

PARKING ON THE EVE OF MORE BAD NEWS

you haven't given into the forty-ounce yet
moaning when you blow on its neck just right
for tonight you make do with skin
for tonight I'm aloe vera stretched over your belly of scars

before love there are doctors
spirits and dead nerves between us
clogging pores, staining our lives like iodine
for tonight we make do with skin

though I know the dosage it takes to light the inside
I haven't given into the bottle yet
moaning when you blow on its neck just right
for tonight I take sips full of wind

if there is more to this cliff
this edge of the world romance
more than dead ends and scarred flesh
let it be found in the stars
a sacred code
charted and passed on for generations
a scroll tucked inside bottle
with news of a lost pair
in search of new skin to love with

ODE TO AN ESTRANGED LAX

Having lost my tribe,
I'd come here seeking Rosa Carmina's face in late night arrivals
someone always hugging, crying, goodbyeing
a census of parallel lives
where any rolling stone could leave at will
stretch arms, tilt hat, wave ticket and take off into the next.

I needed to know you'd never shut me out.

Now we threaten you,
must relinquish all emotion just to stand in line
with no one holding hands
everyone steaming in the ash of an unthinkable fate
pay phone receiver confirming
beyond metal detectors and unexpected frisks
in a land of dormant volcanoes
in a night of fainting blue skies
awaits one sweet melon ball kiss.

UNDER THE BRIDGE

His face a cactus paddle
arms and legs—stumps of an olive tree
the school sent a warning letter
she reads it to the mirror

behind stumps of an olive tree
the boogieman lives!
warnings left in lipstick on the bathroom mirror
she believes someone will believe

the boogieman lives,
in a manila file, under a hundred such files
she believes someone will believe
the girls in their mini-skirts, their faces made-up, shoulders bare to the sun

a hundred such files on a desk held hostage by 2nd class victims
she wipes his spit off her neck
her mini-skirt torn, mascara smeared, bruised shoulders bare to the sun
she claws her skin until there is nothing left

she wipes his spit off her neck
inside the boogieman growing
the red headed nurse holds her hand while the doctor scrapes
          until there is nothing left
under the bridge but a gym bag and broken shoe lace

inside her—an egg covered in spines
a bell rings, freeing an endless trail of 16-year-old girls
pink sweaters and pumas with fat laces
the number 2 bus with stops just after the bridge

an endless trail of girls, most walking home alone
his change swallowed by money slot
the number 2 bus with stops just after the bridge
her scars testimony, the boogie man lives.

EXIT STAGE LEFT

You, my love, are lonely
because we with spray can proverbs
have gradually made their sonnets our own
we their most aggravated wound
have taken this treasured jewel
and polished it with black soap.

You interview the dead on open mics
more secure in spotlights than séances
ask out loud where a brother can score in this town
to weather this tempest of addictions
we tour sketches of sidewalk artists
hold our ears to the wind for news of island babies
survivors of shark-infested seas
landed on jagged concrete of this New Spain.

Loving you is the first hit
lips tight round a glass river
I wonder what we'll make with the smoke and
how many turns each will take before passing?

If life has ever failed you
then know not to plant me in your heart
for I would grow there too fast
pulsing in asthmatic sensitivities
each breath a refugee from the high life
under red velvet of my sex.

My sweet unconditional, exit stage left
no song could save you from the orgy of oxtails and old habits
no summer rain could remove your ink stain from my lips.

HOUR GLASS

I. 1995
From where to where we've come and still so far from home.
I call you to be heard but you are too proud to listen.
You call me to advise but all I hear are the mad ramblings of a woman
who has turned her back on that brown baby
once stuck to her pink breasts.
This routine as much family as physics and bombs
more related than up is to down
more codependent than codeine & flu
I scream I AM through the phone, then hang myself
on the umbilical cord wrapped around her version and mine.

II. 1999
I send slides of my DNA so she can see
there is no way to avoid this life she claims I've chosen
but logic concludes with Hello
instead we discuss musicals
sing a hymn or two from *The King and I*
and for a moment there is harmony
then I remember there are Asian stereotypes
and negative feudalistic subplots to consider
I have crossed the line this time for sure
Hammerstein is choking me and Rogers is breaking through my front door
while she pounds out reasons why I am...
an unfit American, a terrible citizen, my rent late,
my car illegal, my man unemployed, my credit in ruins...
though I can't see the mess I've made
I know she is boiling over and my heart skips beats
because it knows I am no longer her little girl
and that's when we both get the point.

III. 2006
I exit a burning Los Angeles on a magic tax return check
a gallon of gasoline in one hand and pen in the other
for five months she has held in every tear
cause she is Virgo and they don't lose well
even the doctors tell me how competitive she made the last days
a race between her spit and the lymphoma
not even my rage can get me there in time
like her I refuse to cry but there is sand in my chest
in my throat building up into tumors
it takes me years to spell *I am sorry* with single grains
and just seconds for her to sweep them all away.

YOUR ISLAND

nighttime in your mother's bed is a marathon of creed
incessant chirping of coquis
abusive rain on tin rooftop
knowing you'd rather miss your island than own her

in four hours you'll call to say you're not the one
that no mystic could tap the vein to your heart

the choir only hears what they want
your drum calling Eleggua to open phlegmatic chords
hands rough from digging in other men's yards
gently tracing my pink shell
your beard's broken needles scratching
worn 45 of my laugh lines
the slow roll of a homemade cassette
your boleros holding the air hostage like you never left

BLOOD

Your boy asks where you go when you are gone
you point to a black hole only a dead man could see
there son, in-between God's eyes.

Did you think of him when you held out your arm
fist tight green veins throbbing with another punch of anthrax?
Does poison pass from father to son?

While other men saw naked angels
carved in crude oil skies
you saw healthy kidneys
two pair
one for yourself
one for your father
the man whose hands held bottles before they held yours
stumbling up rock past waterfalls and prehistoric trees
he led you up summits of el Yunque
asleep against a stump while you counted stars.

When they called your name did you know how far you'd travel
and what color you'd have to kill?
Did the blood of "sandniggahs" spill into your dreams?

High from a scorpion's kiss at night you'd see Yemaya rise
above the tanks and sleeping men
her hands cupping a turquoise sea
your son at the bottom
asleep on a bed of chicken bones.

Did you own your hate when they told you
there was nothing wrong with your body?
no toxic verve seeping from your hand to his
no pill to keep the grains of sand from filling your lungs.
At the observatory he has his own story for each light
his own reasons to survive
he has found you wounded but willing to ask for his help.

FOR THE FLOWER WOMEN

For years the family has called to tell of deaths that couldn't wait
of flower women who could no longer breathe stained air of memory
women woven of chichicaste and mud, spotted with age
alone in houses loitered by grandchildren
who still feed off sagged breasts
as steam from clay pot clings to their faces
like responsibility of having to feed one more.

The phone call is made by some cousin
who would have been brother or sister had they been closer
tired from the wake and scared to practice their English in post-mortem dialogue
we stumble together through fields of fiber optic cables
as to arrange payment of headstone, scent and color of flower,
          dress of beloved.

My father numbed by distance no longer cries
and so I ambassador to the past he's long-since entombed
navigate the river balanced on a worn cross
bobbing between one shore and the other.

It's the absence of the land that won't let me forget
her hand's ritual preparing té de canela
raised veins rubbing herbs and crèmes into my hair
the women who always had time to *pray first M'ija, always pray first.*

Now lying still, a balsa wood figurine of what I would have been
had I been born before convenience
what we the modern nameless warless childless
generation of cracked bridges are
when no one sees our heads bowed before altars we once mocked
twisted beads between bitten nails, lips tucked under with mumbled penance
feigning faith long enough to know with her dies the kind of woman
who lifts tortillas out of sand, shapes them into hearts
fills our bellies on sacrifice and with a kiss
promises tomorrow there will be more than enough.

THE ROSARY

when we make love it hangs on the bedpost
a noose stained brown by blood
a muddy river's overflow
you hold it when you drive
when we kiss your fist always between our chests
our arteries sense the history and crawl
like vines to touch salvation's erect x

on national ditch day I make us a picnic
cheezits chicharrones grapes
small plastic plates and napkins folded like cranes
a skill you say makes you believe in Pangea

instead our holiday is spent in search of the thin rope
knotted by a blind nun
one for each blip in the flatline that was your life
—you promised Him—her prayers would not go in vain
at sundown I sit on the balcony and eat without you
while you dig through my dirty underwear like Pilate's men
hunting for a trace of flesh in the shroud

ON DEFINING US

ABANDONADO, ABANDONAR, ABAJO
you were gonna teach yourself Spanish
while I was in my Don Quixote lecture
legs crossed, eyes intent on absorbing the "A" section
of my Spanish-English Dictionary
the words you choose to learn

ABANDONADO-ABANDONED, DESERTED
ABANDONAR-TO QUIT, GIVE UP
ABAJO-BELOW, DOWN

abajo tu vives
abandonado y abandono
I thought your curiosity cute
but you were not looking for a new tongue to love with
you were looking for another way to say "I quit."

HOW I LOST MY FATHER TO AMERICA*

He was there for the length of El Bigote's grito
GOOOOAAALLLLLL!
and then just like that he'd fade
into another hour-long patience
awaiting the next great angle
I'd wait with him
2,000 miles away in a sagging futon
watching a borrowed TV
that never received team *America* in full pixel form
hopeful as Cuahtemoc's granddaughter
that someday these cleated warriors would grow feathers
fly back in time to when winners were sacrificed
to when one strike of the stone ball
meant seizure or sudden death
back to when the stake's were too high
to hold my father's attention.

Without notice he stopped calling
on Sundays at 8 a.m.
and again at 9
he stopped calling on holidays, birthdays
and in-between days when he does what men do
when they have been left by their everything.

Thought it was my engagement to a communist
that left him speechless under sable palm
waiting for legitimate grandchildren to call on him to play
reason enough to try him after six months
on Sunday at 8 a.m.
and again at 9.

Listening more to El Bigote's grito
than to my innocuous good news
(como'tas papa) bien bien m'ija

y tu? (bien) okay good I love you
pray to Jesus (I pray dad, I pray)
Good (espera papá tengo noticias)
hum okay I love you Good
GOOOOAAALLLLLL!!!! (bye)

*America is the state soccer team of Guadalajara, Mexico

DON'T MESS WITH THE BULL

La Zona Rosa, Mexico, D.F.

Jesus is the cousin that makes being cousins hard
he's Infante without the mustache
a certified hottie
he is policeman and rebel
responsible and cruel
my ideal man
my adopted big brother

he forbids me to ride
the electric bull lonely and waiting
says only a puta would be so crass
so I wait for him to go to the restroom
tie my skirt high around my hips
and mount the dormant beast

this is for las adelitas! I cry
que viva la bruja, soldada, puta!
with an ay, ay, ay! thrown in for good measure
when he comes out drying his hands on his jeans
only to see me gyrating before the world
his friends making bets on how long I'll last
it's like I've wrangled his balls
he tackles
knocks me right off the bull
into the hay
into his arms

when he puts ice on my swollen ankle the next day
he swears my bruises prove him right
that there are some lessons only a man can teach

THE HOLY TRINITY AS DEPICTED IN WEST SIDE STORY

I like to live in America
Okay by me in America
Everyone free in America

I am Anita, mambo high at midnight
sweaty after a private rumble with a man I'd like to call my own
there are nights he calls for my legs only
hung over balcony like peace flags
then there are nights when I turn a blind eye to the war
only to wake my back a field of landmines & lesions
to survive you must love the fighter as much as the fight
sirens remind of a country that turns boys to assassins
no border could impede his ominous crusade
he's seen his village torched
his brother's tongue cut out
his baby aborted by the enemy's dirty blade
I am a red light salve on a wound America won't claim
but I say send me her newly-arrived vipers and thugs
I want to love them in triplicate.

America
Sweet America

I am Maria, mother of convicted killer
morning dove before God
my wings resting on oak
candles nestled in my hair
I paid for his passage with my body
exchanged his health for mine
paid for his uniform with tithes
saved from the months I was too ashamed to attend
waited up nights to see him stumble in bloody
his Sunday shirt torn
I never taught him to kill, but he learned just the same

before guns there was a mother's love
in line at the market I saw her, the other mother
she threw fruit at me and screamed, "madre del diablo"
I know who took her son and mine
it was the man who sticks needles in
prods them until there is nothing left but acid and black tongue.

America
Sweet America

I am the dress that made you look
that brought you home when you could've been out
when you could've been next
I am the satin on your skin
that asked you to dance with your finger tips not your fists
the curve and line that made you forget
for me you will pray to a God you thought had forgotten you
only he is a She and She is bombshell if you can see her
mother if you'll obey her
sister if you must devote your wars to someone's honor
at the end of night I will spin over you
dead set on delaying the last dance
a parasol of razor blades
a vow of tender flesh
a silk thread around your neck.

GOODNIGHT MOON

there was no moon the night I spent $43.50 in long distance charges
to hear you tell all the reasons I'd already heard
from my godmother my government
on why Cubans and Americans should never meet

there was no light when I left your letters
broken sacraments at the door of the only Orthodox Church
that still believes enough in God to leave its gates open at 3 a.m.

there was no silence high enough to block the celestial hum
the universal "I told you so" ringing like church bells in my hung-over heart
there was no answer no wind no you

I drew what I remembered of your face on the steamed stained glass
a map to where we left our hand prints
like an army of doves dipped in blue paint
enough to protect our nest in Trinidad
where we dared to plant wartime possibilities

your goodbye a reminder
never again will a line be open enough between us
for me to accept collect charges from your particular revolutionary star

LA BELLE BALLERINA

Like Scarlet she will not go quietly
she argues with specialists over words like "terminal" and "treatment options"
her bald head a blotchy map of resistance
the remaining hairs thin splinters of trees left after the Bomb
she pushes the nurse's hand away and promises the doctor this is not over
at home she feeds the cat, talks back to the president elect
she decides what we'll have for dinner, then too sick to join us
she retires to catch the last hour of another American Movie Classic.

In the bed where she read credits as they scrolled over her swollen womb
I catch her laughing
as technicolor lovers fight over who to invite to the ball
I take her feet in my hands
spread the tired bone and skin
massaging reminders of the nights it was her gown spinning
and the world went drunk with her grace.

TOMBSTONE INSCRIPTION FOR
A LOVER ON 115TH

When you left
I never bothered
To take the sign off your back
That read// Recovering addict
Do not disturb
W/flightless
Love things
It would only bring
Bruises//

SIZE 10
for Nehanda

exile in Havana means
your shoe collection retreats into the closet of a Harlem apartment
you once rented when times were good

in your absence we've won
arguments on identity
perched on love seats
sipping ginseng teas
flirting with affirmative action
still sprung on what it's done for us
never stretched far enough to snap back

you'd smile and say *black*
baby, that's all you got
lift your left fist to your lips
and mumble COINTELPRO

photos of your lover, Mario
remind me of JJ from Good Times
his broad-toothed smile has you open
loose like New Years 1979
but in his grip I see you twisted
a squeeze of lime into warm rum
needing love like every woman do
holding tight like every mamma do

Ms. Dalton, I see you fly past in a U-Haul truck
you took four years to find your way to that island
your baby girl crying out for a reason she could touch on
why liberation for the People meant mommy's never coming home

they say you live it
live it like a Cuban
live it like you need it
cause maybe you do
a burst of superwoman
in and out of sweaty rooms
spilling a little secret here or there
so no one forgets what you gave

you Cherí Amour are grandmother to a beautiful ward
she, like yours and the fists before
lost in choices no sane women should have to make
from fifteen stories high you yell *Happy New Year!*

I came here to shop for feet I've only seen run
two for one at Payless
cause mamma you sho'nuff lived up to your size ten

SO AND SO

when we were children
my friend Lisa, the Baptist
told us suicide meant Hell for those who dared
to slice or swallow their way out of His grace
I told her to go to Hell cause my cousin was in Heaven
right where she belonged

when we were children
Charita came to my sleepovers
braided Lisa's hair into cherry-sized knots
and sang us all Bobby Brown's prerogative
in the morning she'd go back to the Southside of town
where Africa had settled 200 years ago against its will

when we were children
Central Avenue might as well have been the equator
slicing through our bicycle routes like crime scene tape
making us as curious as we were scared to cross
over the years we'd grow into strangers
shadows of an original hate
we could not remember why
we were no longer giggles in unison
when corn popped out of kettle into our wide-opened mouths
we could no longer remember when the doors to our houses
became steel plates between the nations taking cover from each other

rumors spread round those who know
you used to know so and so
and so I heard Charita was now a dancer
pumping hard at night
by the dim lights of club Atlantis
where baseball players doubled as pimps
for dentistry students and single mothers

rumors spread round those who know
you used to know so and so
and so I heard Lisa traded in Sunday school
for keg stands and best friends
who all called her whore
when number 54 said it was her with him and number 23
behind the bleachers she'd bleed onto her white pom pom shorts

and when I heard what I heard
I didn't defend the two loose-toothed girls
I'd once told all my secrets to cause I knew
they knew what they'd heard on me too
how I was a gang-girl now
bandanna beat downs to my credit
how I lost my virginity playing spades in an alley
where runaways converged to plan the next 7-11 heist

looking back it's hollow how
we came to trade each other in on slave blocks
outbidding with rumors of masters we'd conquer
someday I'm gonna pop some corn
and send my baby to deliver it on her two-wheel ocean blue bike
to the houses where we used to sleep side by side like sisters

LAUNDRY WITHOUT YOU

bald Colombian men argue over the referees call
how they would have made that shot
these men forced to come to this country alone
sentenced by war to do their own wash
trip over my scattered load
as they reenact the goal with a crushed coke can
the mamacitas with their hair in rollers
laugh extra loud at the pile of egos on the floor

could not tell you the benefits of liquid to powder
or if beige could be teamed with the whites
soon suds consume the room
tios slip, abuelas curse, babies cry
the Filipino manager waves his cane and screams *mamatay dyablo!*
ready to slay the machine with an up-set stomach
now a three-headed monster daring us to come closer

as I bob by the donut store
an empty detergent bottle my buoy
sea foam extended from Elysian to Virgil
I note Chapter 10 in the Illiad of my life without you
is as sad as Chapters 9 and 5
the ones where I tried to wax the car and tenderize the meat
the ones where I slid off the hood down the hill
covered in garlic salt and soy

without you I have no domestic role model
no iron man chef or certified buffer
I'm missing you like San Quentin misses tits and ass
crying into fabric softeners
yeah, missing you like that, damn

TUESDAY NIGHT AT KING KING'S

for two days after I saw you
maraca clave then rum
in your hands I'd sweat lava
working my skin into blisters
I never minded
the mirrors
the ice
never asked where you were before
or where you'd go after
as long as you came

for two days after you sang
sabia que ibas a llegar
I answered each ring
expecting to hear you missed me most at lunch
midday under a bitter sun
still it was enough to dance
under your nose
with his name I've forgotten
how much I hated
hibiscus wilted behind my ear
I'd hear the rumors of your conquests and laugh up blood

pride is an island—more hell then oasis
still I missed you and you knew it
damned I went on dancing
with his name I've forgotten
the exact extent of my rage
framed by your taino afro
challenging gravity
your lips swollen with song
mocking me still
sabia que ibas a llegar

"I knew you'd come" and I did
fists first, you kissed the knuckles
then flame, you lit the candles
then spit, you filled the glasses and toasted our love

tonight the good girl is leaving early
hands full of maraca clave then rum
back steaming from the pace of the mambo
head held high this time
hibiscus coaching
don't look back
and I won't
not even when you call my name
mid-song, center stage
and that is worth the price of admission

TESTED

the pipe sighed before it gave way to the weight of the Federale's boot
long and worn it sighed the way a woman does when her man is explaining
why he must leave we were fifteen miles from the border five hours from
crossing eight from home the activist in me thought it unjust a waste of
a perfect pipe the night before cheap wine and moon Ensenada full of salt-
water puddles the licking between us the jagged line between moon and sea
they wanted me in exchange for your freedom their smiles filled with silver
their tongues forked with the thought of the trade laughing at my white girl
English (the kind I turn on when I most want to know the truth about men)
they made you do push-ups two hundred and thirty-one for each mile we'd
traveled to escape ourselves and the ending we'd promised we'd never let
happen your arms heavy with the weight of your duty to protect the sigh of
your chest under the Federale's boot a reminder that love is not the shadows
we left dancing by the fireplace but a showdown between us and the world

TESTED II

what does it matter, positive or negative
my cells have a secret to tell

what does it matter that I knew you a lifetime or one night
that a simple question could have evaded this wait

what does it matter, when in the moment precious is as she does
and she does what she wants regardless

what does it matter, this endless week at Lammle's, Borders, the page
celebrating the flutter of everyday

what does it matter, the answer
if Eve has already taken her bite of infinite sin
and being great-granddaughter there can be no hope for me

what does it matter, the answer behind that door
in a room filled with Kleenex and cushions
in case I don't take the news well

what does it matter, the nurses are on lunch, all except one
it matters to her that I know before the worry on my fingertips spreads
from one magazine to the next

and what do you care that on the way home there is only Springsteen
and that I've known every word since birth
you can't start a fire without a spark

what does it matter that he's right
or that I've survived another day
having been skipped over by the wild flames

what does it matter when the house of my neighbor will still burn

TESTED III

cacophony — the sound of a 4th grade music class

disingenuous — me the last time I took on a Puerto Rican drummer

harangue — my mother on finding out about said Puerto Rican drummer

fell — he fell my heart like a lumberjack in a sacred forest, no one heard
the crash but me

plunder — I plunder through the sales rack to work through the ache

these words borne by the mouths of men I never trusted
branded into my brain with each repetition
with each florescent flash card
closer to 600

"You must improve two hundred percent to be considered for our program,"
must twist and tame tongue to this foreign vocabulary
this multi-syllabic regime of founding fathers

it's Friday night
the kitchen staff is cleaning
their salsa beats tug at my feet
stuck in the drill of ages
proof of worth
scale of words
Oxford has swollen my tongue
tongue that would rather kiss
spout poems or talk shit
it is 10:35 p.m. and there is no end
to the droning academic klan in my head
I deny them their last words, reclaim my day
and slip away in grooves on the floor

WHY I LEFT WITHOUT SAYING GOODBYE
for Ebony

my thesis on the teachings of Ghandi was left on the Greyhound
between Cambridge and Port Authority I'd let that prayer go
cornrows half in-half out, must have scared a few
laws of nature say, a lioness cannot be arrested for protecting her young
but the warrant was written anyway

at Harvard it's illegal to leave your hot comb on the stove
to play Tupac before noon or after six it's illegal
to eat out, laugh loud, ash your cigarette on the pretty red brick
jagged and awkward as two county beds we dared to stay on
but there were too many martyrs that summer
ghost fists eager to punch holes in hallowed halls

still see you in the mirror,
can sometimes feel your hold on my thick mane
wonder where you are and who you've trusted
if you ever left the Brenton Harbor projects again
swore it was all good so why Harvard burn still
in my chest water fountains soothe the public
and thirst is still free, ivy league burn bridges
but we   we   throw   bricks

PUNCH LINE

I. Meyer Lansky – the name of the Jewish Mafioso we couldn't remember at 2 a.m.
II. Muhammed Ali – a hero we can both claim
III. brick walls – why my head always aches after leaving you

After a night of you & Jack Daniels
a dream of myself in a chapel with Meyer Lansky & Muhammed Ali
brick walls topped with elaborate paintings of Heaven & Hell
dare devil anarchists suspended in a cockleshell
pace the room to find a crack in the wall
a million questions gather behind my teeth;
like how many angels did they see at the bell?
is there an afterlife after the fall?
could I walk away with my guard down?

Subdued by the steady stream of blue river above
the sneering red river below
Muhammed Ali, Meyer Lansky and me
sit suspended on wood chairs like lions
waiting for the punch line to crack its whip
we take turns saying the show will go on.

So this is love just before the straight jacket
the sting operation before your number's called
this is the hull of my heart throbbing with afterwords.

ON THE VERGE OF THE NEXT RIOT

the monster grill of a Mac truck in your rearview could cause panic

my lover is driving for the first time since he hit a tree
and took a well-deserved nap

it soothes him to know I know the songs on 93.1,
the classic *classic* rock station

how Pink Floyd & lasers suit me fine as Prince & pink lace

we agree the children still don't need no education, what they get
from concrete is enough

we interrupt this broadcast to bring you breaking news
on the Donovan Jackson case

a hung jury

another black boy beat down

two white cops balls big enough to cheer from their pews as if
taken by the Holy Spirit

education is winter on his auntie's TV screen

a faded buzz of more to come

valley of smog pierced with high wired toothpicks set up to receive
cell phone soliloquies

a halo of radiation 10 miles wide

20 million microwaves and me with one weak heart

tell it on the mountain, I'm on the road—again,
with a man who can't sing but sings still

tell the black boy, hands tied behind his back, face against the police car
reason has interfered

the city burns to burn behind us, it's desire channeled
by the matches in my pocket

will the willing pay $2.50 a gallon to turn back

at the next exit I cry for the aunties on their plastic sofas, the police
"just doing their job," the long- horned trucker
bullying his way through it all

OBSERVATION NOTES FROM THE NEW WORLD ORDER

Psst!, psst, psst!
Is anyone there? Anyone listening?
Someone looking? Even a heart?

SUBCOMANDANTE MARCOS

MISSING

"...for men must work
and women must weep
and there's little to earn
and many to keep
though the harbor bar be mourning"
—Charles Kingsley

Juan Abrego misses his wife
when he steps off the metro
and just before the wind hits his back
he can feel her breath on his fingers.

He misses his country
the green mountain
the stoic trees
the neighbors and their animals
underfed and overworked he misses most
the little girl with eyes as black as his
who smiles in her sleep
the swinging hammock
the sprawling song of his father's farm
field of corn where they first made love
the child bride and groom
he held her hand and promised not to take long
the vow between them sewing together the hours.

Today Juan Abrego wrote his first paragraph in English
my wife has eyes like twin stars
he has begun to translate the loss
how you say extrañar "missing"
how you say solo "alone".
Juan misses chasing the crows off his land
the uncles gathered to watch the game
a rock he touched everyday on his way home.

But, good luck does not reach this far.
You have to return to its source
my wife has skin like honey
my daughter is a dancing sparrow
the letter is read to the class
then sent with a crisp hundred dollar bill
each with their own envelope to fill
the life they left
the lone woman sowing the field
the black eyes hiding
the child grown tall as the stalks.

IN MONTAÑITA OLD AGE IS A GIFT

for the victims of crossfire

there are days when the daughters think to sit on the porch

sip the same lemonade

a brew of what's gone sour in life

instead they stay in

hold babies tight to their chests

it's best to lie still

pretend you are dead

so when the beast comes

he can roll you over

maul your face til it's a monster's mask

leave you wounded but living

to be old as Maria & Ismenia

you must survive more changes then men

they'd been friends since the rivers ran blue

spirit twins too busy reminiscing on first loves

to notice machine guns aiming at air

how Armando made love with a flower first

sending blood to her hand her arm her shoulder

how her lips trembled

yes, it was like that with Pedro

a jewelry box after only two months

the lock carved from alabaster

shock made her drop it

the gold ring calling to her from bits of wood and shell

he never got mad once in 56 years

they laid side by side

they'd escaped the violence so many times

found refuge in fields and churches

an endless string of prayers wound around each fist

taking watch over children's children

shooting goals between trash bins

it was milk she needed

for milk she sent her grandson to the store

maybe she knew to save him

glasses shattered

sunshine turned dusty rose

their lives mixing again

two swallows

struck down by skipping stones

CHRISTMAS DINNER 1997

The martyrs of Acteal have opened our eyes ...
they left us the truth as an inheritance ...we see
how there is no justice in Mexico ... we see how arms
have come to our communities ... and are given to
assassins ... all to strengthen an army that never tires
of taking over our lands and controlling our
populations."
　　　　　–From a statement made by the
　　　　　Abejas at the year anniversary of the massacre

we sit heads bowed
praying over an obese turkey
three snow white heads
and my brown mane
grateful to our Lord
for more stuffing more meat more gravy
light and dark we sit
juxtaposed like negatives

they chatter   avoid my eyes
I am *hysterical,* liberal dead weight tied to their North Star
each a Jeopardy contestant speaking with endless expertise
on campaign finance and the *corruption* of welfare
they chew unaffected by the ten-second news flash
on another massacre below our stretched first world belt

excuse me

I search suburban streets for the remains of fifteen harpooned placentas
fifteen mothers not given a choice between their lives or their children's

excuse me

alone in a strip mall parking lot
I mumble prayers for forgiveness through the filter of my black-n-mild
as visions of reckless machine guns dance through my head

excuse me

mother, it's true
I've never mashed the molcajete with their daughters
never carried my children through jungles deep in the night
vines tearing at my face
bouquet of fear trail enough for monsters
to bound close behind for five days

it's true   I was born here
not under their piece of sky
but that does not stop their faces
from burning like champa in my corneas
their screams from bursting my ear drums

tragedy does not pause for Christ's birthday
sadness is memory
of when time began
gave birth to man
and man took his hate
shot it into his shadow's heart
saying take that   take that   take that

NEW WORLD NEWSIE

Your village in El Salvador had no school
but you made it to 2nd grade anyway,
took a mountain path past five encampments
to stand at your desk and recite the tenets of the latest leader.

Farmer Diego brought paper from the city
a peso a sheet, pounded as thin as Mayan gold.
Once you sold your boots for a book
and the captain tied you to a tree for a week.
Oh, what kind of soldier you would have made
had you stayed on to see the revolution through.

Mr. New World Newsie, can you read the trouble you sell?
Nowadays fifty cents buys a world of pain.
You stand two seconds too long, daring the red light to go green
willing business men in sedans to drive through you.

You shove Spanish news—more blood than truth—in their window
switch hands and try English—more words than art—on the windshield
headlines stain your hands and sleeves.
Can you explain why so many don't want to know?

"Good" & "Evil" went to war today. Where's the news in that?
Once you miscounted your sales and they docked you a week's pay,
still you stood at Fairfax & Adams waiting for someone to ask your name.

HORIZONTAL GEOGRAPHY LESSON

your bed is the edge of the world
where we lie
unnumbered
unhinged
tracing the outline of your United States map

you're determined to know the state capitals and their order
rainbow quilt of stoic rhombi
how free the coastal states
their furthest seams defined only by volcano and sea

my index finger trails the Rio Grande
its mud bleeding down my chest
your thumb leaves coyote tracks
guides for those that follow

this land is ours

as the politicians sleep through our rebellion
we take back California for my grandfather
Louisiana for yours
here manifest destiny dare not brand its legend
arrows pointing toward an imagined west
a muted south a lonely east a frozen north

all trains are caught still
no freeways flap close enough to wake us
this night reparations are collected in pores
opened by mutual love for a fifty-first state
free state shape of waning moon or twin bed
state with only room enough for two

AT THE JAPANESE MARKET

tangy seaweed salad
hiccups, sandals, straw mats, sweet egg
eel unraveled
longan like small investments
solitary lunchers
griddle, slurp, clanging plastic udon bowls
the endless noodle the elder will not cut
as if it were a lifeline to her mother's home in Nakasato

ground pearl crème, rice, steaming ginger tea
to trick the skin into an enduring youth
her leg kicking under the table
a nervous condition brought on by her husband's death
left foot tapping to the REM song,
this is the end of the world as we know it
a thin silver hair poking tear duct of her right eye
like salmon bone demanding attention

as a girl she was told this country was the end of the world she knew
she nodded
said nothing
what more was there to understand

mochi stuffed with red bean paste
wooden chopsticks, wasabe in a tube, pickled quail eggs
one thousand silver fish with their eyes intact
video game carjacks
a flutter in her chest
poster for a war movie peeks out from behind the sticker machine
under the bomb a fallen star pear
she squeezes, bruises it,
slides it into her purse before anyone can see

she remembers the weather man telling her today there would be sun
her umbrella knows better
eventually the noodle chases its own tail
the antsy knee will shatter when she falls
the star pear will wither into a heavy coat of loose skin
ever sweet but too worn for market

CANVAS LA

In a room occupied by carpet stains and a short white dog
we sit afflicted by colds brought on by evening runs through sprinklers
Marley's blues bob through air like soothing cough drops
as we practice minute speeches
each one of us a wind-up doll of nuclear facts
for primetime we flyer promos of guerrilla tactics
ask microwave masses to break habits of corruption
we promise there is still time to save this planet, your soul, your dog
there is still strength to stop boulder of apathy
don't let it flatten our dignity
we look deep into stigmatized eyes and say *I trust you*
to deliver your letters of intent to the doorstep of Congress
respectfully require them to uphold humanity
praise their constituents with sweet rains of democracy
tomorrow is growing in your granddaughter's belly
we know you are willing ready able
to open your wallet and make a difference.

CANVAS REDONDO BEACH

nativity on his shingle roof
World Wildlife sticker on his counterpane
Berkeley print stretched across his chest
he answers with jaded breath
what do *you* want
I qualify
I want what *you* want sir
taxes spent on life affirming initiatives
education & health care
not nuclear weapons
protection for...
You murdering bitch!
open door slammed shut
I slam right back
you sir are an extinct beast Berkeley would gladly 86
and Christ, well, he would never bless your rooftop or your front door

FROM THE BACKSIDE OF EL TEMPLO DEL XOL

Teotihuacan, Mexico

tourist don't dare wander behind this sacred prism
where eagles swoop and lizards boast crimson swallows
vendors tired of lowering labor into pesos
bow to avoid eyes of modern day Dons
their arrogance carved with flanked hearts into spine of maguey
names deep as linoleum print of conquest
now pressed into jerseys and sweats
what is left on the backside
are cement sheets painted with blood
segun los guias who use every tactic
to seduce gabacho wide eyes into big tips
above us prayers float in on drunken hummingbirds' wings
sudden and free they parry a millennium of tacit questions
but all I want to know is if we can blend into this ancient compass
make love like serpentine statues
twisted as wild flames on this shadeless day
and get away with a little conquest of our own

ON THE ROAD TO SAN CRISTOBAL
DE LAS CASAS
Chiapas, Mexico

Can you sleep with a semi-automatic in your face?
this is first class baby
reclining seats no chickens the bathroom door stays closed
Terminator I & II on the screen

Where's your passport?
the barrel fits into the canal of your neighbor's ear
four men escorted off like bleating calves
the bus driver continues on

Where's your birth certificate?
in your underwear drawer in your tia's house
in Colonia del Valle about 12 hours north
You are American?
American by birth?
And your VISA?
"I'll be back" the sergeant says and you know
he has seen the movie before

What to do with a pocha on the bus?
What to do with Guatemalans lined up alongside the road?
too many to turn back
too pocha to turn in
a ballpoint pen bribe
nail clippers and a tin of Godavi chocolate
the family will understand
it was me or the truffles
the truffles they say

say goodbye to the Danes
suspected socialists
and the German hippie with only one shoe
the bus driver takes a sip from his flask
what'd I tell ya, this is first class baby

you take a sip too
ask what else there is to watch
something to make us laugh a little

and there from his cabinet he pulls a cassette
of all that is wound right in the world
a Cantiflas video, "Romeo and Juliet"
silly love, man versus his own comic timing

our nerves melt with laughter
abuelos children surviving members of our international load
hyenas in the high mouth of this mountain god

the next stop isn't so bad
even the militia can't help but watch
from the corner of their eyes—a smile
reminder of when Mexico owned Hollywood
la Epoca Dorada, the Golden Age
when a short man with big ears and pouty lips
turned his people to the politics of survival
that is the politics of laughter
contagious as the politics of fear

WOMEN WITH WALK

para las mujeres del Isthmus de Tehuantepec

fast in stride
don't slow down for strays or splinters
earlobes stretched with swaying gypsy lanterns
baskets of jicama on their heads and tissue between breasts
should they have to pee somewhere deep in the Sierra Mixe
they don't wait for sunburnt tourists to begin the bargain race
they take what they ask for nothing less

breaking into rivers
eucalyptus strapped to their back
moon in their belly
a child on each hip
they slip into and out of this isthmus
unaccounted for by any government census

broad and strong
don't waste time on faith
they prefer stone
carved in times when what was   was
they brush their teeth with blood
paint their nails with wings of market flies
as their children steal bread from men
who haven't been home to eat in ten years

stretching our earth's crevices
balanced on torn feet
they spit back sand into sculpture
lungs full of iguana teeth
all the while outlasting famines
feminism and non-profit foundations

BASIC TRAINING

Miguelito writes *Viva Zapata* in dust collected on the van
his fist size of an over-sunned tangerine
in my Bruce Lee camouflage
he tells me I look like *watcho*
watcho?
watcho.

machine gun simulation
of government watchmen
he hides at the river
dares me to jump from a log draped in algae
double dare?
double double dare.

from here you can hear training drills
sharp turns & loading clicks
hand-in-hand
a wasp scares us into action
better to belly flop then be stung
the war paint washes off
his worried look gone young
a smile that says I've completed basic training

BASQUET

a lesson in Tzonzil math

10 fingers of red clay
spread across a midday sun
an impossible shot

14 skirts of black wool
chase and praise each other
ponytails up by one

28 arms for carrying wood and guns
wave for a chance to shoot
love passes love delivers love scores

history is boys waiting
taking their turn on sidelines
eyes fixed on the lassoed god

OLMEC HEADACHE
Jalapa, Mexico

fat face
squint nose
stuck in shadowed showrooms
just begging for a kiss
I see you Father
and I spot you
two thousand years in exchange for this...
that you might grow
Botero wide arms legs and chest
wobble through *their* cities of glass and wire mesh
dig through *their* modern graves
taking from them only the best
with which to start your own museum
now with *their* babies skulls encased
laugh us up an earthquake
and put an end to this nosy race

PALACIO DE BELLAS ARTES
Mexico, D.F.

Inside walls hiccup colors
brighter than Bubble Yum
bursting from Tonantzin's lips
her laughter bouncing off polished tile
as billfold politics call on her to scream
in a million shades of red
this new Mexico is rational!

outside street clowns billow flames
in the shape of plumeless eagles
awing atheists and taxi drivers
in between green lights
face-painted oil barons
mouth with singed lips
this new Mexico is rational

in Maria's Internet Café
arthritic commies sip tea while masked
teenage rebels mass email IMF secretaries
a virus that reads... this new Mexico is rational...
fwd: this new Mexico is rational...

en Estadio Azteca beggars in bleacher stands wave
row by row they cheer on Red Cross nurses
Chicadee boom a la bim boom bah!
Que viva este nuevo Mexico...
Rah! Rah! Rah!

at los Pinos* there are logs
covered with drumlines of devoted termites
served in tacos to children with silver teeth
each with a cleaning uniform that reads
Juan, first son of this new Mexico

in hallowed halls there is comedy
a drunken skeleton of Tin Tan
making love to his left palm on opera night
an endless flicker of florescent light
reveals prayer slips stuck with wads of gum
to the under seat of velvet chairs
dios mio este nuevo mexico es...

in the gift shops there are oxygen masks
and thirty-pound books on Orozco, Siquieros and Rivera
their mistresses chaperoned by robot slaves who flip the pages
an endless stock of postcards advertise
this new Mexico is rational
this new Mexico is rational
stamped and sent out on trails of volcanic smoke
inside swirling ribbons tickle marble slabs
all clean enough to eat on

outside the hunger for edible paint goes on
untamed by the good press

* *los Pinos is the presidential residence in Mexico City*

102

CHINESE NEW YEAR IN HAVANA

dragons dare drunks to dance on rooftops
lovers twist egg noodles on chop sticks and kiss
between bites bodies drift in with offerings of ron y rice
there is fire in some eyes
distant memories of a land not surrounded by time
long brown legs tight like husked cane
wide hips gripped by callused hands
exiled panthers, pardoned poets and madmen
thumb prints that leave no trace
history burnt off to protect them even here
they share scars and indiscretions
their children tuck fortunes into seashells
passed back-n-forth on the crests of West Indian waves

POLISH
Sancti Spiritu, Cuba

we break into earth one stab at a time
our work song *Sancti Spiritu, Sancti Spiritu*
our harmony careful
we may be sisters but we are still strangers

with the patience of a midwife the ghost of Celia Sanchez watches over us
her fingers long rays of sunshine tilling ageless universal matter

woman here have perfect nails
painted in garnet, corvette, cinnamon red
none chipped, none dirty, perfect-perfect red

all I have are nubs
bitten stumps where my womanhood would be if I'd let it grow
I show my mentor Lourdes my hands and look to where the pigs are slaughtered
she doesn't say a word
which I know from workshops
means there's nothing nice to say

below folds of earthworms are cut in half and I am torn
between letting her know how hungry I am or digging deeper
her laugh unveils my dilemma
taking off her gloves she says, "tienes algo pa'esconder"
nervous because I do have something to hide
even those in solidarity can be a danger to a nation floating outside the box

our last day together
I present her with two new shades
copper/silver–pennies/nickels
loose change planted in the soil of a country
that hasn't forgotten its promise

PORT AU PRINCE

a choir of ebony angels sang on both sides of the plank
leaving thumbprints on my temples
mosquito bites burnt into my sides

as tall as their steel drum
I swayed to its hollow call
wanting to be wielded smooth like that

children sprinted alongside the bus
climbing I wore matching yellow shorts and shirt
a giraffe on the chest and visor with straw bill

some could not stand the guilt
their dollars waving from windows
the barefoot hunger jumping like Go Fish

I did not have to give
but my mother she carried plastic grocery bags
filled with old clothes sandals tennis that no longer fit

the road to El Citadel a wound chambered nautilus
my donkey led by the boy with a gum green watch
that played Chopin's Minute waltz at every quarter hour

when he held my hand to help me down
I knew he knew I loved him
would have held his hand the whole way

but there was a bus to catch, parents watching a five star dinner waiting
a whole nation to attend to
far more hungry than my budding breasts

TRAVEL GUIDES
Verdadero, Cuba

The cock of a modern Master is only hard at dawn and dusk
for twenty minutes a day she congratulates him on his conquest
the rest of their time spent on the balcony of Hotel Paradisus.

Friends from nursing school gather to observe
their respective dates sipping pink drinks by the verandah
off-duty they practice names of body parts in Latin
there is a test next week but one sits quiet
busy with daydreams of pigs bled in her uncle's field
six short corpses drawing nothing but flies.

In the morning she lies still long enough to feel the sweat from his palm
sink into the warm cave between her thighs.
He never knew her name
did not ask her age at dinner
or when she danced for him on jagged parapet of El Morro.

She has been his docent for a week
guided him through the old and new of Havana
translated the menu, taken his pulse, lotioned his back
all to feed her family meat for the month,
buy a bicycle for her brother Leonardo,
who paints naked women on palm fronds—their silhouettes
left to dry in the sun,
and a TV for her oldest Victor
who spends his days cleaning hotel rooms
where he can catch the latest steps broadcast on MTV.

She gossips with her godsister Tita
on local men caught with their pants down
her godsister Tita who has walked this tightrope longer
and can say her alphabet in German, Dutch and Portuguese
her godsister Tita who believes revolution costs nothing
but what you are willing to sell.

GRASS
Squaw Valley, California

I. Sergio pushed the insatiable mower singing Frank Sinatra's
My Way in broken English he did not notice the white moth
caught in swinging blades or his abandoned cigarette
sparking a patch of dry matted grass
with a rubber sole meant to last him three winters he put the cherry out.

II. It took the brothers ten years and 3,500 golf courses
to save enough to bring Doña Lydia here and now that she's home
she sits staring out the window of their single room apartment
dreaming of an uncut green like the one in Lacandon.

III. When you blow on it just right you can set an Andean flute free
postcard of a time when sheep ruled and our only duty
was to play them to sleep with songs of cud and endless campo.

IV. For $5.25 a square foot you can buy a patch of evergreen shag
lady on T.V. says for 59¢ a day you can feed a starving child
I write a check for six and send a letter to my congressman
asking for an increase in home improvement taxes
enough to stretch a football field across the cracked earth of Somalia.

V. Underneath cleats, bent reeds of garden grass are sending out a call to arms
through subterranean telephone wires there is talk of a movement
to take on these overgrown larva with their driving ranges and grazing tanks
to rise up fourteen feet in a day and tame them into lesser beings.

WINDOW SHOPPING ON BROADWAY

Downtown, Los Angeles

she stares at her reflection in the window
a showgirl's figure superimposed
on her own round silhouette
her huipil is stained with red clay
black birds dance across her chest
their caws fending off men
who lean in with *mamacitas* and *bonitas*
their accents and beer steaming the glass

there is no harvest of wool here
no poppy seed dye
crushed red grasshopper
no loom between her legs
here women's feet press cold steel pedals
their sewing machines hidden
behind garage doors here women
dress their worn fingers with band-aids

at the ends of each arm
she sees the palms that once shuttled rainbows
the lines of yarn held tight to the loom
she remembers the rug underbid
by another weaver two stalls down
and her grandmother's plum-stained hands
waving to clot the bleeding sky as her bus pulled out

betrayed by their own uselessness in this new world
her hands press up against the warm glass
beyond her reflection a rack of leopard print
pants suits cut to hug a size six
calling on her to begin the day
in someone else's body

CLEAR GOLD
Imperial Desert, CA

one gallon
two lips
split by a river of endless thirst
hot flood of desert paint
washes off silt semen sweat
and when you arrive
there will be no paradise
just beef jerky
bile and an endless mile to go

a silent rock
balanced on the head of another
a look out cross warped horizon
its every layer touched by the devil's shaking finger
rippling tide of sand
and no man no woman or child
shall be forgotten

five gallons
ten split lips
the thirst of an emptied sea
ravine of shoes and shit and silence
a cactus field of winter roses
shell and somewhere
a young girl carries a water bottle to gym class
an expectant mother fills the dog's bowl
a tired waitress brings her table fifteen cups of ice
lemon margaritas on the rocks
slushies
fountain drinks
courtesy cups
an endless mile to go
twenty-six gallons
fifty-two cracked lips
split with the gush of air

an opened promise
between Rock Mountain and the Arco station on US 2
51 blue flags swarm
desert flies
awkward and bumbling in an alchemist's wind

change is uncertainty of the mind
menace of sanity melting
with each surge on the thermometer
107...108...110 points of lava
walking on hot coals
the endless mile behind you

two water towers sliced
a bloody foot stumbles
between this world and the next
a fever
a succulent plant
a sunrise on stilts
a pair of waning eyes
two cracked lips
a sip of clear gold

RIPE

City of Industry, Los Angeles, CA

sing her a song
a merengue line
a slip on glove
made of lace not plastic

marry her to the fence on Alameda and Manchester
where she stands under parasol of circus colors
cutting symmetrical wedges
coconut cucumber mango mamey

fingers red with chilé
lips a cracked slice of watermelon
tight from salt sticks dipped and sucked on
a desert survival trick

she reads the license plates of each passing car
writes them down in a code no MIT prodigy could break
it is the language of ancestors
glyphs used to transfer an entire civilization to an unknown plane

the clean-up of precious fruit takes ten light changes
two pairs passing in each direction
a steady gutter growl of Broncos and Mactrucks
exhaust of two-ton machinery clinging to her shoulders neck back

in La Ceiba she would make plans for Fridays
be dressed for Club Luna Llena by ten
a DJ and a tent wide enough to set sail for a warless country
her worries dampened with the ardor of good times

today she's too tired to plan such freedoms
the Bandamobile passes Umpa! Umpa! Umpapá!
a reckless toucan blaring
memories of her life before red lights

HE'S GOT THE WHOLE WORLD IN HIS HANDS
San Francisco, CA

black lung flip mop rock breath
swabbing the seams
you see the whole world from here
your own roof in the Mission
the man picking steak from his teeth
the trolley falling back
and Reverend Moss picking his scab in Golden Gate Park

the wind creeps under your hard hat
she whispers *war is on,*
it's an election year,
you'll never know how much they need you
good people of this city
disgusted by your squalid hands
your eternally-black nails
the smell of tar tainting their tranquil day

this morning your daughter
remembered to wash her hands
waiting outside the restroom door
you hold her backpack
cold damp of pipe water
steaming between your palms
as you walked her to class

MERIENDA
Sancti Spiritu, Cuba

women talk over scores of last night's domestic disputes
their nails spread petals of poinsettia
no car no cell phone no house
they own only their loves
wrap themselves tight in them
licking and smoothing the edges like cigar rollers in El Laguito

as we graze on green tomatoes and stale bread
they dissect the latest novela broadcast from Brazil
as they chew and chat
inhale Popular cigarettes
we pick up enough attitude to know the subject is men

city girls we click in similar tongues
how we left our men behind
to travel to school to taste other lips
they laugh, say our men are thick veins in the sides of our necks
throbbing reminders of how weak we can be

what doesn't translate is our pride
an overfed capitalist trademark
the Ego thinking it can do it all, alone
how far we are from love they say
from the surrender, we should be so lucky
to know when not to let go

UN BESO SURREALISTA PARA LAS CINCO
Y PUNTO DE LA TARDE
Madrid, España

Pedro the Cruel has left his jockstrap hanging in the window again.
Cousin Dalí is tanning hides on the rooftop
while Cirque du Soleil cast members play
olley olley oxen free in the garden maze.

North African hustlers slang mix tapes to museum docents
while I sip malt beer to chase down sardines and eggs.

On the way to see the King
I stain *la Güernica* with red lips meant to survive sex
they take me away in a cloisonné egg
to where Señor Lorca is hard at work
digging his own grave on the roadside of this new republic.

What would it be to die for your land your lover your goat?

I chip in, ask what he has planned for the afterlife
he answers, *heaven is making whoopie in the cobalt sands of Atlantis.*
drunk with port stolen from the liquor cabinet of the Queen
we brave the sea, only to drown just out of reach of Asmodea's rock.

CHRISTMAS SHOPPING IN MADRID

slick black leather   strapped to the backs

     of brujas   from Goyas' final days

dark as a moth eyes   they smoke chains around their lungs and mine

timing my move   I dare   to break   their shopping routine

each sucked in face   an excuse   not to give me directions

so who told Columbus   which way   how did the boy

ever find the palace   with all this pushing

and shoving   for gold   did he wander   for days

choking on the people's lack of concern   no wonder

               the man would land so lost

PISCINA PACIFICA

PELIGRO!
NO SWIMMING!
still the three-year-old china poblana goes in
to hide from the water monster
her father, un pelon con seaweed locks
tattooed from his neck to his ankles
with a map of forgotten urban planning districts

a few waves away, surfers, really accounting execs
meditate on spiked hair of Lady Pacific
I have seen her swallow three strong men on a day like this in Manzunte
their boards spit out like toothpicks
from here She's just another calculating club trick
reeling in cholos and cotton swabs alike
her hunger does not differentiate
bones boards bravado
it all goes down the same

oil derricks to my left accent the shit refinery to my right
my mother's voice says it's crude to call it what you want
it's still paradise's bidet
PELIGRO!
my big toe split by a Bud bottle, half full
I want to know why there are dead ladybugs in the sand?
Do islands have feet that tickle the sea floor?
And if high tide is ever ashamed of her lows?

CHILD OF QUESTIONS

*"Live your questions now, and perhaps even
without knowing it, you will live along some
distant day into your answers."*
–Rainer Maria Rilke

in between the underwear ads and the text of the presidential address
there is the question only a child would dare ask   *why*
in 1941 it cost 5 cents to print the compound equation of all our doubts
six generations later there are still no answers

we appear cleaner than we did yesterday
our hands tied to the remote
we watch shrapnel burrow in an endless desert
an engineering student seared *live!*
the school of mud walls collapses *live!*
a maidservant's lung perched on bayonet *live!*
our perverse uncle burnt in effigy *all live!*

child of questions sing sweet reason
make of your eyes reflecting pools
catch them at their windows
stop them mid-sentence
barking into red phones
their tongues barbed with this nonsensical language
its rules always bending to make way for exclusion
child of questions fight off your ABCs
block print apathy A B U
Abu Haider is taping his windows
he will stand alone to defend his bookstore
his daughter's questions ringing in his head

fifth graders down the hall spin 50 Cent
cause they gonna get rich or die trying
the war drum is bouncing down Hoover in a 67' Impala
red and white stripes whipping from the chrome rims
child of questions driving uninsured
his sagging-jean resolve to get back at The Man
a wardrobe not afforded peace of mind
the terminal *why* scraping cement

TWIN TOWERS
Downtown, Los Angeles

At first glance you look like any other office building
streamlined conveniences; mauve wall, vending machines,
manicured trees

you make it seem easy to enter friendly for visitors
and then at the red light stray eyes stare too long
wondering how any business man or woman
could enjoy a room with no view
slight tease of window a diabetes test strip

if we were to prick your walls with seismic pins
open your slants enough to let light in

how many stones would fall loose? how many elephants would
charge through?

ODE FOR THE MIC

for The World Stage, Leimert Park, LA

through time you stand a shepherd's staff
herding profits and derelicts
heroes too
souls intent to do right by the world
under red light
spit in your pores
an obelisk dipped in honey
you stand to make love
like stela in Copan
resurrecting history with each voice

I've seen men catch seizures after just one dance
hurling through their concrete façade
I've seen you make them cry
still they come back
with whooping cough confessionals
in solemn whispers
in eloquent rage
the pay off is hearing their name called

you are Pied Piper's flute
Trinity's anchor
Moari spear
Jacobin's bayonet
San Andreas faultline trembling
Liberty's backbone aching
thermometer rising
bass string pulled tight
playing the scales of our breathing
our over-heating
our melancholy brand of new world jazz
an antenna calling all channels home
and when the city burns again
you'll prove descendant of Black Eye Brahma
digging center to where sanctuary waits

and when the bombs drop too close
you'll turn pole vault
lifting us over and out of despair

and when they finally discover the dissidents
planning revolt in your lair
you'll turn Katana blade

til death you'll stand
and should that day come
we, the poets, will have our own Iwojima
raise you from the soft skin of death
to your rightful post center stage   all eyes on you

THE DAY I HUGGED SONIA

for Sonia Sanchez

a thousand bobby pins
jumped from the island virgin's hair
as she read of white petals and cosmic touch
heart to lung
a chorus of katydids sung
with Sonia suddenly the Muse seemed noble and fair

the day I hugged Sonia
the streets of South Central held an impromptu parade
in her honor children spun ribbons around streetlights
maypoles and madrigals
there was dizzy joy
bubbling up from the shanties of Santo Domingo
and in Quahiniqualapa black was beautiful again

the day I hugged Sonia
atheists took to forgotten maps in the stars
only to find their families waiting
at Union Station beggars were anointed
with Frankensence and Myrrh
the Earth shook along its laugh lines
and the pen in the hand of the White House
could not hold still long enough to sign off on war

the day I hugged Sonia
a monsoon of good will struck my right cheek
and being reborn I could not fight back
a window opened in my chest
a feverish pot of rice and peas thrown out
a desperate need to feed the world
to scratch and pull at the scalp of freedom
until it tingled with possibilities
and it would be naïve to think
she felt such things in my humble embrace
but she would have had to been blind

to not see the smile on God's face
when Sadako's paper cranes turned flesh and feather
lifting cataracts of smog from the pupils of our estranged cities
able to see for the first time
people gathered in parking lots to dance under an ultramarine sky

the day I hugged Sonia
a life time of poetry didn't seem so long
didn't seem long enough

INDIA

for the children of Shaw, NE, D.C.

you were seven
the world ancient
everyday you took the globe home in your backpack
as if it were a basketball or bundt cake
you took it out to show others
this is where we are — right here
that spot is home

the day the tanks came to 6th & S
you wanted to welcome the men on duty
"they're here to help," you said and took them sweet bread
while we, the grown folk, stood behind the gates of fear and contempt
they smiled at you, dropped their aim to the floor
you took out the globe
showed them the spot
you told them they were home
and for that moment they were

that summer our block was red, white and blue
with blood and flood lights
police cars and sergeants
the war was fought while we ducked under tables
16 deaths under the age of 21
you made cards for the mothers
with a picture of the world and a star
lingering above the words "this is home"

I knew then you were not of this Earth
still I clung to your geography
you made it seem the world wasn't so heavy
and with enough sugar you could change
the aim and intentions of men
you were seven
the war ancient
still you carried us all
in your backpack they found crumbs and a compass
directions home should we be lost without you

IN THE MASTER'S YARD
October 16, 1995

We hang like voodoo dolls above the masses
only today there are no nooses
it is before Islam is a flaming pitch fork in Grant Wood's hand
before we land on Mars
before even dust.

Maya Angelou is rising from pulpit
a floating soulful Buddha
first lady of healing
her minister of music, Stevie, can't see the masses
but he knows them by the smell of sandalwood and sweat
one man for each hair standing on his back

today the scars of the whip
heal with balm of brotherly love
oils and incense burn
today, you say "Al salaam a'alaykum"
like you've been saying it all your life
like you mean it
cause you do

from the trees we descend
mixed hued girls with no roots
there's no one to tell us to go home
and if they did we wouldn't know which way to run
lost in a mist of vendors
marking the date with commerative plates and pens
tomorrow the news will say 50,000
but proof is in your pictures
shots of rolling waves
under a perfect mesh of cloud and light
framing a million promises made this day

man to man
man to woman
man to mirror
it is before you become mother to an endangered species

before my godson will learn the burden and blessing of his brown skin
before hunters have had their fun with him
Mr. Farrakhan approaches the mic with his swagger step
and though no man is perfect
you can see if the possibility exists it is here
in the smile of the son on his father's shoulders
listening as if his life depended on it
cause maybe it does

it is before I throw your bad choices in your face
and you say, my problem is I thin my poems
make me immune to my own vices
like the drug dealer I've imported from back home
who has cone to be made "man" among men
he looks lost, bronze faced with sun-bleached dreads
Malcolm T-shirt on and Africa medallion
Unity bandanna and cowry shell ring
he has converted
he is sorry
and tonight will bed down
with no thought to the clients
feigning for him to come home

forgiveness is a prayer mat at the Capitol exit
an underground railroad
and all are free to get off
stroll past Master's house
picnic on his front lawn
Salat and sunset
lawyer, mailman, preacher, beggar
of humanity let them say this
there was a day when hate was chased from the Hill
fearing the free would riot and tear the hallowed halls down
and when there was only prayer and hope to accuse them of
the masses stood guilty of believing change would come

BOTTOM OF THE NINTH

There are no pedestrian crossing signs in Tikrit

red eye target running so low

Lt. Gomez shot

and if war were turned inside out

if it was your life or theirs wouldn't you have done the same

                                           a boy running

                                           towards home

towards goat herd

a tin roof haven

a good man would have aimed lower

soldier, today you are God

let no child be left behind

the few. the proud. the brave.

dressing wounds

cameraman watching

12 billion eyes are on you

Lt. Gomez shot to protect his patrol

and if it was your life or theirs wouldn't you have done the same

(this material may not be suitable for children under the age of 12)

still, the eyes of the world can not look away

a 40 inch flat screen at the Burbank airport

suits sip Stoli, Heineken draft

diet Pepsi and pizza lodged in their molars

"Put the Dodger game on!"

today Lima is God

a shutout

the boy stuck between bases and a small tin haven

a field of goats

child with one run to go

his father's walls face west   he did not see his son fall

the sand in Lt. Gomez' socks

a pillar of regret on the chopper floor

Lt. Gomez declined to speak to the cameras

bottom of the ninth

all bases loaded

Lt. Gomez cradles the boys head

a last breath

a last hit   a foul ball

but who's keeping score

"I learned about life
from life itself,
love I learned in a single kiss
and could teach no one anything
except that I have lived
with something in common among men,
when fighting with them,
when saying all their say in my song."

From "Ode to the book"
Pablo Neruda